ELIZABETH THE QUEEN MOTHER

10/01

Mobile

ELIZABETH THE QUEEN MOTHER

A TWENTIETH CENTURY LIFE

Grania Forbes

Chivers Press • Thorndike Press
Bath, England   Thorndike, Maine USA

This Large Print edition is published by Chivers Press, England, and by Thorndike Press, USA.

Published in 2000 in the U.K. by arrangement with Pavilion Books.

Published in 2000 in the U.S. by arrangement with Pavilion Books.

U.K. Hardcover   ISBN 0–7540–4052–6   (Chivers Large Print)
U.S. Softcover   ISBN 0–7862–2310–3   (General Series Edition)

The text of this Large Print edition is unabridged.
Other aspects of the book may vary from the original edition.

Set in 16 pt. New Times Roman.

Printed in Great Britain on acid-free paper.

British Library Cataloguing in Publication Data available

Library of Congress Cataloging-in-Publication Data

Forbes, Grania.
      Elizabeth, the Queen Mother : a twentieth century life / Grania
      Forbes.
            p.   cm.
      ISBN 0–7862–2310–3 (lg. print : sc : alk. paper)
      1. Elizabeth, Queen, consort of George VI, King of Great Britain,
      1900– 2. Queens—Great Britain—Biography.   3. Large type books.
      I. Title.
DA585.A2 F67   2000
941.083'092—dc21
[B]   99–048323

To Mark, Edward, Matthew and George

CONTENTS

ELIZABETH
THE QUEEN MOTHER

CHAPTER ONE

A SCOTTISH LASS

The year was 1900, the dawning of a new era and yet vestiges of the previous century lingered on. The disgraced playwright Oscar Wilde lay dying in Paris, the obstinate Boers were soon to be trounced but not defeated at Ladysmith and Mafeking, the Australian Commonwealth was about to be proclaimed and Lily Langtry was about to be exposed by the American press as the Prince of Wales's mistress, as she played the part of a dissolute heiress in Washington. Strenuous efforts were being made to 'solve' the continuing Irish problem and the trade unions had decided to abandon the 'Liberals' and form their own 'Labour' party. Long-distance buses had started operating (the journey from London to Leeds took two days) and a new drink called Coca-Cola was launched.

Queen Victoria, who had come to the throne in 1837, still held sway at Buckingham Palace but, now aged eighty-one, she was beginning to fade. Her nerves, frail at the best of times, were further stretched when a fifteen-year-old anarchist made an attempt to shoot the Prince of Wales during a visit to Brussels.

Into this changing world came a girl who was destined to achieve greatness comparable to the old Queen and, like her, become a beloved national institution. Her name was Elizabeth Angela Marguerite Bowes Lyon, the ninth of ten children born to the Earl and Countess of Strathmore. She arrived with the minimum of fuss on 4 August when the weather was so hot that horses were forced to wear straw hats and débutantes had to abandon that fashionable new dance, the 'cakewalk'.

Just where she was born has been the subject of much debate but modern historians now agree that it was in

London and not, as previously supposed, at the family's Hertfordshire home, St Paul's Walden Bury, Indeed, in her passport, issued in 1921, her place of birth was clearly stated as London. The mystery arose because her father, a sweet-natured but absent-minded man, was six weeks late registering her birth and only dashed into nearby Hitchin to record her arrival at the Bury two days before her christening. He was fined 7s 6d for being so tardy. However, eighty years later, the Queen Mother proudly announced that she was born a Londoner and then refused to explain further saying 'It is of no matter'.

Several theories have been put forward for the mix-up. One theory is that her mother, then aged thirty-eight, was advised by her doctors that it might be wise to book into a nursing home for the birth as it was seven years since her last pregnancy. At that time it was not the 'done thing' for aristocrats to use such places and it might have been decided that once the child was safely delivered, mother and baby would be discreetly driven to their country home.

Another possibility is that Elizabeth arrived rather suddenly as her mother motored down from London to St Paul's. This would account for a local doctor from Welwyn, whose practice lay on the route from the capital to the country, proudly telling his family that he was present at the birth and would explain his subsequent invitation to her wedding.

Perhaps the most probable explanation is that the baby's father simply could not face a hot and tiring journey to London to register the birth and chose instead to nip down the road to Hitchin. He may have felt that his little white lie was of no consequence and indeed it would not have been but for the fact that his youngest daughter would one day be Queen. Certainly Elizabeth's arrival did not cause a stir. Her paternal grandfather, the 13th Earl of Strathmore and Kinghorn, did not even mention her birth in his daily diary.

The baby was born into one of the oldest and most distinguished Scottish families. On her father's side, the Lyons could trace their ancestry back to the Picts who fought so valiantly against the Romans, and descended from King Robert the Bruce.

The Bowes part of the name had arrived in the mid-eighteenth century when a Durham heiress married into the family. Her mother, Nina Cecilia Cavendish Bentinck, was equally grand. Had she been a boy, she would have become the 6th Duke of Portland.

However, for all their lineage, the Bowes Lyons were not a stuffy lot. Theirs was a large and happy tribe which consisted of May, who was seventeen when Elizabeth was born, followed by Patrick, Jock, Alexander, Fergus, Rose and Michael. When Elizabeth was twenty-one months old, David arrived to complete the family. Her eldest sister, Violet Hyacinth, had died of heart problems brought on by diphtheria aged eleven, seven years before Elizabeth was born.

Lady Strathmore was the keystone of the family, so admired and adored by all her children that she never needed to punish them. A gentle word of reproof was enough to shame them into obedience. As one of her daughters recalled, 'Mother was a very wonderful woman, very talented, very go-ahead and so upright. She had terrific sympathy: the young used to pour their troubles out to her and ask her for advice, often when they would not go to their own parents. She was extremely artistic. She sewed lovely embroidery, which she designed herself. She had an extremely good ear for music. She would go to a concert and listen to a piece of music, and then come back and play it perfectly.'

Lady Strathmore was not only adored by her children but also by the household servants. A housemaid, who later became Lady Elizabeth's dresser when the staff were hard pressed, remembers an occasion when she smashed a valuable antique. 'I was cleaning out the drawing-room after a weekend house party and moving the screens round the fireplace that kept the draughts away. What I didn't realize was that there was a precious vase on a plinth just behind one of them. Anyway, as I moved one of them, to clean under it, there was a sickening crash. I pulled it back and there was the vase in a thousand pieces,' recalls Miss Monty. 'Well, I thought I was going to get dismissed and when I was summoned by the butler to Lady Strathmore's room (she was ill at the time) I was certain of it. She was sitting propped up in bed. I thought, "Now I'm for it" but to my amazement, she put out her hand towards me. It was covered in beautiful diamond rings. She said: "I hear you've been in the wars, Mabel. I am so sorry. Accidents will happen. It was only a Ming," And that was it. I nearly fainted but that was just like her or so the others told me. I hadn't been there for very long, you see. She was the most

7

wonderful employer and we all loved her.'

However, Lady Strathmore was no libertarian when it came to her offspring. She imbued them with the maxims normally found on the samplers children embroidered in Victorian times. 'Duty is the rent you pay for life,' was one of her favourites. Another was 'Life is for living and working at. If you find anything or anyone a bore, the fault is in yourself'. It was a motto that Elizabeth would carry with her for the rest of her life.

Like her husband, Lady Strathmore was deeply religious. Church parade and daily prayers were as much a part of daily life as eating or sleeping. It was this faith that enabled her to try to cope with the grief over the death of her eldest daughter, Violet, and later the demise of Alexander, who was killed by a brain tumour following a cricketing accident at Eton. Nevertheless, Lady Strathmore was not a conventional Victorian mother. Unlike other

Countesses of her time, she refused to hire a wet nurse for her babies, preferring to feed them herself. Her offspring slept for the first eighteen months of their lives in a cot at her bedside and she supervised every detail of their daily lives. Although gregarious and a wonderful raconteuse, she was rarely absent from home and while undoubtedly loyal to the Crown, she scorned snobbery and the social round that endorsed it. She was once heard to quip that 'some hostesses feed royalty to their guests as zoo keepers feed fish to seals.' She was also unusual in that, at a time when most aristocrats and royalty treated their children as third-class citizens to be given the plainest of everything, Lady Strathmore made sure hers had the best. This even extended to the nursery where, according to her granddaughter, Lady Mary Clayton, the décor could have graced the grandest drawing-room in the land. 'My grandmother was of the opinion that children, however small, should be surrounded by fine things so they would learn to love and appreciate them. The nursery at the Bury was no exception and had lovely furniture and beautiful paintings. I remember the walls were covered with Miacchis which were exquisite pictures of mythological legends or religious scenes. They were very like the illuminations in an old manuscript. The painter was a good friend of my great-grand-mother, Mrs Scott, and lived in Florence.'

Lady Strathmore also brought a touch of Tuscany to the highlands of Scotland. Over ten years she created an Italian garden in the grounds of Glamis Castle where Elizabeth, nicknamed the 'merry mischief', and her 'bruver' liked to play. All this made a great impression on the young Elizabeth and to this day the Queen Mother not only has exquisite taste but an enthusiastic passion for gardening.

Elizabeth's father was a much more down-to-earth character. His favourite garb was an old coat tied at the waist with a piece of twine and his favourite occupations were lopping trees and digging ditches. He was frequently mistaken by visitors for one of his farm labourers and offered a swig of whisky to keep out the cold. He also had the slightly eccentric habit of going out in the middle of the night to collect fallen branches which he would chop into kindling in his study. When asked about his nocturnal activities, he would reply that it was the only time he could get 'a little peace'.

Lord Strathmore shared his wife's passion for music. His own father had written choral works and trained his twelve offspring as a madrigal group. He loved to recite from the classics and was an expert on the Bible. He also never failed to complete the *Telegraph* crossword. His great passion, however, was cricket and games against local teams were taken seriously—particularly the annual needle-match against the Dundee Drapers. When he achieved a hat trick of three wickets against them, his jubilant team bought him a new Panama hat.

Such was the piety of Lord Strathmore's father that he had practically bankrupted the estate by building Episcopalian churches throughout Scotland. The consequence was that Elizabeth's father spent much of his lifetime paying off the debt and had to sell land. This meant that the family were not well off by the standards of the time and Lady Strathmore's account book shows what a careful housekeeper she was, Every item of expenditure, down to the last bar of soap, is recorded. Indeed, it used to be a joke among the tenants on the estate that when they heard shooting, they knew that a dinner party was planned at the Castle. 'They needed the game, you see, for the table,' explains old retainer Jock Scott.

It was in this Edwardian world that Elizabeth was brought up. When she was a month old, her mother employed Clara Cooper Knight, the daughter of a tenant farmer at Glamis, who was to serve generations of the Strathmore family. Always known as 'Allah', because it was the nearest that the children could get to pronouncing Clara, she was the archetypal nanny—gentle but firm, very professional, very loyal, extremely efficient and serene in even the most difficult circumstances. She also adored the children and they her. She describes the young Elizabeth as 'an exceptionally happy, easy baby, crawling early, running at thirteen months and speaking very young.' Soon Elizabeth's constant companion was her brother, David, and the two played together like twins. Raiding the larder and begging sweets from the cook were favourite occupations as was pouring 'boiling oil' from the topmost turret of Glamis, ninety feet up, onto unsuspecting visitors below. The 'oil' was in fact icy water but it had the desired effect. Other pranks included taking villagers 'hostage' until a ransom of sweets was paid or upsetting the chauffeur by putting a foot-ball under the front wheels of the family motor car. When the poor man engaged the clutch, there was a loud explosion which nearly gave him heart failure.

When down south at their Hertfordshire home, St Paul's Walden Bury, Elizabeth and David had a secret den in the old ruined brew house in the grounds. They found their hiding place while searching for a stray bantam and had christened it the Flea House for reasons that became only too apparent. It was there that they would skip their morning lessons to smoke the cigarettes and eat the chocolate they had acquired by devious means while a frantic Allah searched for them in vain. The older Strathmore children complained that their younger siblings 'got away with murder' and even the Countess had to admit a certain indulgence to her 'two Benjamins' as she nicknamed them. As she once sighed when faced with an implacable Elizabeth, 'I pity the man you marry because you are *so* determined.'

However, sometimes despite protest, what Mother said went. Guests had to be entertained and the pair—David dressed in a jester's costume bearing the Strathmore coat of arms and Elizabeth in a dress copied from a Velázquez painting—used to perform the minuet as their dancing teacher, Mr Neill, skipped ahead in his heavy brown boots playing the fiddle. The visitors found it enchanting but to the children it was embarrassing.

Like other young ladies of her generation, Lady Elizabeth, as she became after her father inherited the Strathmore title in 1904, was educated mainly at home. Initially it was Allah who taught her the basics of reading, writing and arithmetic but soon governesses were employed including Miss Laurel Gray. Lady Strathmore asked Miss Gray to keep an account book of the children's progress. 'When they were good, a good mark and a penny. And, of course, a bad mark was shocking,' she recalled. 'Elizabeth wasn't too good but she always got a good mark. She was naturally a good scholar. A bad mark made no difference to David. I was as strict as I could be but he was terrible!'

Elizabeth quickly learnt to read and at an early age 'devoured books'. Initially she liked stories about animals but soon moved on to tales of chivalry and adventure, passed down by her older brothers and sisters. History books particularly intrigued her and she was fascinated by atlases showing the different countries of the world. From the age of six, she and David had a series of French, and later German, governesses, and she was fluent in both languages by the age of ten, Also on her busy schedule were piano lessons and dance classes not to mention a personal art tutor. She had inherited her mother's musical ear and was the star performer at a school concert when she spent two terms at the Misses Birtwistle's Academy in London. Her ever-indulgent mother had sent her there partly as an experiment but also to cure her loneliness after her brother David was sent to preparatory school in Broadstairs. The loss of her companion hit her hard. As she wrote to a friend, 'David went off to school for the first time on Friday. I miss him horribly.'

However, Lady Strathmore decided that Elizabeth was better educated at home and more governesses arrived to continue her education. In June 1914, Lady Elizabeth sat the Oxford Preliminary Local Examination and passed all seven set subjects with flying colours. They were Arithmetic, English History, English, Geography, French, German and Drawing. A few weeks later, the First World War was declared as she sat watching the music hall on her fourteenth birthday—and her education effectively ended.

While Lady Elizabeth was being cosseted, some might even say spoilt, by her family and friends, her future husband, Prince Albert Frederick

Arthur George, second son of the Duke of York and Princess Mary, later King George V and Queen Mary, was having a very thin time of it.

Born in 1895 on that dreaded day of mourning, 14 December, the date when both Queen Victoria's adored Consort, Prince Albert, and her beloved daughter, Princess Alice, had met their maker, it was not an auspicious start. Even his christening had to be postponed because of the death of his great-uncle, Prince Henry of Battenburg, spouse of the Queen's adored youngest daughter, and the forerunner of men who would shape the future of the British monarchy (his great-nephew was Lord Louis Mountbatten).

Despite the Duke of York's trepidation at telling his grandmother the news, 'Gan-gan' reacted favourably saying, 'I have a feeling it may be a blessing for the dear little boy and may be looked upon as a gift from God.' He further ingratiated himself by offering to call the infant Albert and making Queen Victoria his godmother. She was so delighted that she commissioned a bust of his saintly great-grandfather, Prince Albert to be made as a christening present and wrote, 'It is a great satisfaction to us all that it should be a second boy and I need not say how *delighted* I am that my great wish—viz. that the little one born on that sad anniversary should have the dear name of *Albert*'. To her disgust, her own heir (Albert Edward), although always called Bertie, had made it plain that he would never be called King Albert the First and eventually became King Edward VII.

She was also aware, as was the leading newspaper of the day, the *Morning Advertiser*, that 'an heir and a spare' was essential given her own experience. While her eldest son, however much she disapproved of him, might still be alive, she had lost the next heir—her grandson Albert Victor—who died of pneumonia soon after his engagement to Princess Mary of Teck. The Queen, finding no other suitable bride, married Mary (who was known as Princess May) to Albert's younger brother, the Duke of York, who later became King George V. As Frances Donaldson comments in her biography of Edward VIII. 'It was a matter of chance, though a happy one, that the Duke of York was, by character and temperament, the more suitable both for the Crown and to the tastes and affections of his future wife.'

For their first seventeen years together, Prince Albert's parents lived in York Cottage on the Sandringham estate in Norfolk. Described as 'a glum little villa similar to those found on the outskirts of London', it was a rabbit warren of very small rooms and narrow passages. It constantly stank of stale cabbage, there were not enough bathrooms and the Duke of York himself commented that he supposed the servants must sleep in the trees.

The Duke was by nature a martinet, neat, punctual and hardworking. He led the life of a traditional country squire and spent most of his time shooting. He was irrationally proud of his family and the slightest infringement of his rules, real or imagined, would throw him into an apoplexy of rage. He was not above putting his boys over his knee to smack them and even his 'adored May' got the rough edge of his tongue, silently leaving the table when she could stand his rudeness no longer.

On his fifth birthday, Bertie received a letter from his father. It said, 'Now that you are five years old, I hope you will always try to & be obedient & do at once what you are told, as you will find it will come much easier to you the sooner you begin. I always tried to do this when I was your age & found it made me much happier.' There was no birthday present, no birthday party—not even a card.

Bertie's mother was a strong and purposeful woman but lacked the maternal instinct. By nature extremely reserved, she was incapable of showing overt affection and left the upbringing of her three eldest children, Princess Mary having been born a year after Bertie, to a nurse. The woman is widely described as 'sadistic and incompetent' and ended her days in an asylum though not before she had made the royal children's lives a misery for many years. Mrs Christina Stringer was the maternity nurse at Sandringham and she told her daughter-in-law of the horrors she witnessed at York Cottage. 'She told me that the nurse was so harsh and so strict that the children had a worse life than any of the village youngsters. She used to hit them with a big rod for no reason at all and never cared for them at all. They weren't even properly fed,' says Mrs Mabel Stringer. 'She was particularly cruel to Prince Albert because he had a stutter and had temper tantrums but the more she hit him with the rod, the more difficult he became. She was dreadful to him. According to my mother-in-law, when she vented her anger on him with the rod, he would just cower away and hide himself.'

Her favourite charge was David, later King Edward VIII and the Duke of Windsor, but she was so jealous of him possibly forming any sort of attachment with his parents that she would twist or pinch his arm so hard that he would scream in agony when he entered the drawing-room. This led his mother to believe that her son could not stand the sight of her and the children were hastily bundled back to the nursery. 'The sobbing and bawling this treatment invariably invoked understandably puzzled, worried and finally annoyed my parents,' the Duke of Windsor recalled in his memoirs. The nurse's reign of terror only ended when a brave nursery footman reported her activities to the Duke. To their astonishment, he and the Duchess discovered that the woman had not had a day off in three years and that their children were suffering from rickets, a disease normally associated with the half-starved children of slum dwellers. Later Bertie had to wear splints to correct his knock knees and his stammer worsened when a private tutor forced him to write with his right hand.

However, the Duchess of York's sense of fun surfaced when the highly repressive influence of her husband was removed. 'When he used to go banging away for a week or two on some shoot in the Midlands, and my mother would never go to those things, we used to have the most lovely time with her alone—always laughing and joking down at Frogmore or wherever we might be—she was a different human being away from him,' remembered the Duke of Windsor. When the boys served their French master tadpoles on toast as a savoury, their mother was highly amused. 'My father would have been furious. She liked that sort of thing when she was alone with us.' Another bonus was that Bertie was a natural athlete and shone at sport. He outplayed his brother on the golf course and hunted with the West Norfolk Hounds. He learnt to skate when the lakes at Sandringham froze and was a star at football and cricket. He and David would organize teams to play the local boys from the estate.

Despite a struggle with maths, Bertie passed his examination to Osborne and entered the Royal Naval College just after his fourteenth birthday in January 1909, a year before his father was crowned King George V. He found the life hard and lonely and within six months he was sent home with whooping cough. Although he came bottom (or very nearly) of his class, he entered Dartmouth two years later. Within a month both he and David caught mumps and measles, and their condition was sufficiently severe to warrant bulletins in the medical journal, *The Lancet*.

Desperate to serve his country, Prince Albert was thwarted by ill health, which plagued him throughout the First World War. First he was rushed ashore to have his appendix removed, then he experienced acute stomach pains and had to be given a desk job at the Admiralty—a sinecure where he became bored and restless. Finally his pleas to be returned to his ship were heard but within three months he was back on the hospital ship and declared unfit for active service. Despite protests from his father, it was not until May 1916 that Bertie, debilitated and depressed, returned to his ship, the *Collingwood*. However, his moment of glory was at hand. The Battle of Jutland was about to begin and at last he was 'able to get at the enemy'. He describes it vividly.

'I was in A turret and watched most of the action through one of the trainer's telescopes as we were firing by Director, when the turret is trained in the working chamber and not in the gun house. At the commencement I was sitting on top of a turret and had a very good view of the proceedings. I was up there during a lull, when a German ship started firing

26

at us, and one salvo "straddled" us. We at once returned fire. I was distinctly startled and jumped down the hole in the top of the turret like a shot rabbit! I didn't try the experience again ... My impressions were very different to what I expected. I saw visions of the masts going over the side and funnels hurtling through the air etc. In reality none of these things happened and we are still quite as sound as we were before. No one would know to look at the ship that we had been in action. It was certainly a great experience to have been through and it shows that we are at war and that the Germans can fight if they like.'

Having finally seen action in the front line, Prince Albert's confidence rose and he was able to brag to his older brother, 'When I was on top of the turret, I never felt any fear of shells or anything else. It seems curious but all sense of danger and everything else goes except the one longing to deal death in every possible way to the enemy'. In a later letter to David, he is in more philosophical mode. 'In a war on this scale, of course, we must have casualties and lose ships & men, but there is no need for everyone at home to bemoan their loss when they are proud to die for their country. They don't know what war is, several generations have come and gone since the last great battles.'

As Prince Albert's official biographer, Sir John Wheeler-Bennett, notes; 'In a single summer afternoon, he passed into the full dignity of manhood.' Sadly that was the end of Bertie's war. A duodenal ulcer was diagnosed and, after several periods of enforced rest, he underwent a successful operation in November 1917. The following year he was transferred to the Royal Naval Air Service in France, just two weeks before the Armistice was declared.

While Bertie was battling the Boche and his chronic ill health, Lady Elizabeth had been just as busy tending the sick and injured at Glamis Castle. No sooner had war been declared than her brothers joined up—Patrick, Jock and Fergus serving with the Black Watch, and Michael with the Royal Scots. It was also a time for weddings. On 17 September at Buxted in Sussex, Fergus married Lady Christian Dawson-Darmer and a week later the family rushed north to Scotland for Jock's marriage to Fenella Hepburn-Stuart-Forbes-Trefusis. Patrick was already married to Lady Dorothy Osborne, the daughter of the Duke of Leeds, and Michael, being only twenty, was considered too young to contemplate matrimony.

The nuptials over, Lady Elizabeth, with her mother and sister, Rose, headed for Glamis where the castle was being converted into a convalescent hospital. Red Cross volunteers helped them move beds into the dining-room and billiard-room in readiness for the wounded but Lady Strathmore insisted that as little furniture as possible be displaced as she wished to make the castle homely. She instructed her family and staff that the soldiers should be treated as 'honoured guests' and made to feel welcome. As Lady Elizabeth told her biographer, Lady Cynthia Asquith, 'During these first few months we were busy knitting, knitting, knitting and making shirts for the local battalion, the 5th Black Watch, My chief occupation was crumbling up tissue paper until it was so soft that it no longer crackled to put into the linings of sleeping bags, Lessons were quite neglected.'

The first of the wounded arrived from Dundee Royal Infirmary in December 1914 while Rose was training to be a nurse at Bow Hospital in London, so many of her responsibilities fell to Lady Elizabeth. Above all, she carried out errands and was forever running up the mile-long drive to the village to buy tobacco, cigarettes and sweets for the men. She took photographs to send to their families and helped them write letters home as well as taking them on at poker and billiards. There were even noisy and bloody rat hunts in the crypt. The war-shattered veterans took the little girl to their hearts and a battered autograph book from those days survives. One entry speaks for all. It reads,

*'May the owner of this book be
Hung, Drawn & Quartered.
"Yes."
Hung in Diamonds, Drawn in a Coach
    and Four.
And, Quartered in the Best House in
    the Land.'*

W.H. Harrop of the 8th Seaforths little knew how prophetic he was.

In September 1915, Fergus returned to Glamis to celebrate his first wedding anniversary and see his baby daughter for the first time. Days later he returned to France where he was killed in action at the Battle of Loos. The whole family were grief-stricken but Lady Strathmore took the death particularly badly. For a while the running of the castle hospital was left to Lady Elizabeth and her sister, Rose, who had returned from

London.

In May 1916, as Bertie was fighting valiantly at the Battle of Jutland, Lady Elizabeth was a bridesmaid when Rose married William Spencer Leveson Gower at St James's Church, Piccadilly. Although Rose returned to Glamis for brief periods thereafter, responsibility for the hospital fell heavily on Lady Elizabeth's shoulders. She was also anxious about her beloved mother and would wait nervously on the castle steps for the postman—just in case any more bad news arrived. And arrive it did. On 3 May 1917 Lord Strathmore telegraphed Rose, who was in London with her mother and expecting her husband home on leave, to break the news to his wife. His telegram from Glamis read: 'Michael missing April 28. War Office will wire further news. Tell mother they say not mean necessarily killed or wounded.' However, hope began to fade as strenuous enquiries failed to locate Michael's where-abouts. Only his youngest brother, David, who appeared to be gifted with second sight, was adamant that he was alive.

David Cecil, an old family friend, recalled a conversation he had with the fifteen-year-old. 'He lunched with me one day, and I pointed out to him that he should not wear coloured clothes and a coloured tie so soon after his brother's death, "Michael is not dead," protested David. "I have seen him twice. He is in a big house surrounded by fir trees. He is not dead, but I think he is very ill, because his head is tied up in a cloth."' David was right. Michael was a prisoner of war in Germany, where he remained until his release in 1919.

Another drama also befell the Bowes Lyon family during the First World War. In September 1916 the central keep of the castle caught fire while the soldiers were out at the cinema. Lady Elizabeth promptly rang for help from the Dundee and Forfar fire brigades as well as the local Glamis station. She and David then set about organizing everyone into a chain, passing buckets and jugs of water. When a large water tank in the roof burst, they managed to divert the flow away from the drawing-room and rescued much of the valuable furniture, pictures and antiques. Lady Elizabeth's resourcefulness was credited with saving the castle from burning to the ground and she was toasted with 'Highland Honours' in every house and cottage for miles around. As the local paper, the *Dundee Courier* put it, Lady Elizabeth 'was a veritable heroine in the salvage work she performed even within the fire zone.'

Although the war ended in November 1918, it was not until the following year that the hospital at Glamis finally waved goodbye to the last of the soldiers. Many never forgot the kindness they had received from the young Lady Elizabeth and continued to write to her for years afterwards. However, that was for later; now a mature eighteen-year-old, it was time for Lady Elizabeth to have some fun.

CHAPTER TWO

FAMILY FIRST

The Armistice found Prince Albert cooling his heels in the comfort of the British Embassy in Paris with his old friend, that 'perfect topper', Surgeon-Lieutenant Louis Greig, whom he had first met while a cadet at Osborne. During the four years of the war, the Prince had only managed to serve his country for twenty-two months and it was therefore thought politic that he should stay in France for a while to deflect any potential criticism from those who had lost loved ones in the conflict. As his older brother, David, wrote to their mother, Queen Mary, 'Bertie can be far more use in this way than sitting in England where he has spent most of the war, not that this was his fault! But by remaining with the armies till peace is signed, he will entirely erase any of the unfair questions some nasty people asked last year as to what he was doing, you will remember.'

Bertie spent Christmas away from the rest of the family at a Spa in Belgium where no doubt it was hoped that the curative waters would further improve his health. In the spring, he represented the King at the victory celebrations in Brussels, his first major royal engagement.

It was during the festivities that Louis, the Prince's private secretary, bumped into James Stuart, who was hanging around waiting for his men to be demobilized and was the younger brother of an old friend. John Stuart and Louis went back a long way. They had been at Osborne and Dartmouth together and Louis knew James slightly. Since he and Bertie were almost of an age, Louis asked the young Major to show the Prince around and give him a good time. They went to the theatre, dined at the finest restaurants and took in the sights. It has even been suggested by some that the Prince lost his virginity at this time, which given James's sophistication and fondness for the company of women, might not be surprising.

As James recalled in his autobiography: 'He [Prince Albert] was young and did not want to stay in the Palace all the time. Thus, a few of us used to organize small parties and dances at The Merry Grill for the entertainment of the young Prince. We had a great deal of fun and I got to know the Prince quite well.' The Merry Grill was a smart restaurant and night-club, frequented by James who 'woke the place up' on New Year's Eve by bringing in a couple of his pipers. 'We had a lot of fun in Brussels and I grew to love the place. The small restaurants provided excellent food and Burgundy, but it was expensive and I soon found to my horror that, in a few weeks, I had spent all my war savings for four years.'

The Brussels encounter was to prove a turning point. When it was decided that Bertie should go up to Cambridge University and needed an equerry, Louis' thoughts naturally turned to James. The penniless third son of the Earl of Moray, having tired of studying for a legal career, was only too happy to accept a post in the Royal Household.

Meanwhile, Lady Elizabeth had just turned nineteen and was emerging as one of the prettiest débutantes of her generation, having been presented at Court at Holyroodhouse Palace during the King and Queen's summer stay in Edinburgh. She joined the normal round of parties, dances and outings to the Henley Royal Regatta and the Ascot race meeting. The family's London home at 20 St James's Square was the scene of almost nightly dinner parties and chambermaids made a brisk living passing on billets-doux from a host of admirers.

Weekends were spent at St Paul's Walden Bury where tennis, cricket and croquet occupied the 'bright young things' whenever they were not slipping off for quiet walks in the house's magnificent grounds, which were dotted with statuary, pavilions and ponds. Otherwise the group moved from one great house to another for weekend house parties. August found them in Scotland for shooting and the Forfar Ball where Lady Elizabeth never lacked dance partners. James, who had been at Eton with her brother Michael and served with him in the Royal Scots, was invited over to Glamis in the summer of 1919 and a year later Bertie followed, naturally accompanied by his equerry.

Mabell, Countess of Airlie, a close friend and neighbour of Lady Strathmore and lady-in-waiting to Queen Mary, said of Lady Elizabeth, 'Her radiant vitality and a blending of gaiety, kindness and sincerity made her irresistible to men.' Her dancing was so admired that she was awarded the accolade of 'best dancer in London'. Although the pair had met at a children's party, when she was five and he ten, it was not until May 1920 that

Lady Elizabeth caught Bertie's eye. She was dancing with James at a ball held by Lord and Lady Farquhar in Grosvenor Square. He called his equerry over and asked to be introduced. As he confided to Lady Airlie, he had fallen in love that evening 'although he did not realize it until later'.

However, the Prince had stiff competition. Despite a chronic shortage of suitable young men after the devastation of the First World War, Lady Elizabeth was surrounded by eligible suitors. There was Prince Paul of Yugoslavia, a close friend of her brother Michael at Oxford University, who was so keen to win her hand that, according to servants, he spent hours ingratiating himself with her mother, Lady Strathmore hoping that she would persuade her daughter to accept his proposal. There was Lord Gage, immensely rich and the owner of Firle Place, a magnificent Tudor mansion in Sussex. 'Poor Gage is desperately fond of her,' noted the diairist Sir Henry

'Chips' Channon. 'In vain, for he is far too heavy, too Tudor and squirearchical for so rare and patrician a creature as Elizabeth.' Both the Earl of Airlie's older sons were smitten, the younger Brucie wooing her by dancing on table tops while playing the ukuelele. Another faithful admirer was Sir Arthur Penn, twelve years her senior, who remained one of her most trusted friends; he served as her treasurer all his life and poignantly died the day before he was due to retire.

And then, of course, there was James. The Prince's equerry was a man of dashing good looks who had led a similarly adventurous life. He had run away from school to join up, while under age, at the beginning of the war and had distinguished himself on the battlefield, winning one Military Cross at the Battle of the Somme and another at the Battle of Arras. Described as 'drop down dead handsome', he never had to make the slightest effort to attract women. His take-it-or-leave-it attitude was irresistible and a raised eyebrow or a half smile had them captivated. James was also extremely witty and enjoyed nothing more than rather risqué banter, particularly with a pretty girl. He loved to tease and be teased, a trait he shared with Lady Elizabeth. The pair were increasingly seen together, particularly after James broke off his engagement to Elfie Finlayson, the daughter of a prosperous Glasgow trader. Everyone wondered if they would marry.

Meanwhile, Queen Mary had noted her younger son's interest in the beautiful débutante. During a carriage drive, she commented to Lady Airlie, 'I have discovered that he [Bertie] is very much attracted to Lady Elizabeth Bowes Lyon. He's always talking about her. She seems a charming girl but I don't know her very well.' 'I have known her all my life, and could say nothing but good of her,' replied her lady-in-waiting. It was now understood that she would act as royal marriage broker and as she relates. 'Soon after that the Duke and Lady Elizabeth started dropping in at my flat, on various pretexts, always separately but each talked of the other, She was frankly doubtful, uncertain of her feelings, and afraid of the public life which would lie ahead of her as the King's daughter-in-law. The Duke's humility was touching. He was deeply in love.'

Lady Airlie's counsel to Lady Elizabeth was that love 'would grow' with marriage. However, when Bertie proposed in the spring of 1921, he was refused. Lady Airlie wrote to Lady Strathmore that 'the Duke looked so disconsolate. I do hope he will find a nice wife who will make him happy.' Lady Elizabeth's mother replied, with some prescience, 'I like him so much and he is a man who will be made or marred by his wife.'

Elizabeth and Bertie remained good friends and continued to see each other as yet another season progressed. Gradually their friends married. Lady

Lavinia Spencer and Lord Annaly, Helen Cecil and the King's private secretary Alec Hardinge, and Mollie Lascelles and the Earl of Dalkeith. Bertie remained adamant that if Lady Elizabeth would not have him, he would marry no one else. The Queen decided to travel north to judge Lady Strathmore's youngest daughter for herself. Lady Strathmore had been ill for some time so it was Elizabeth who was waiting on the steps of Glamis to greet the royal party as they drew up on 9 September 1921. As ever, she was relaxed and charming and impressed Queen Mary with her poise and knowledge of history, something very dear to the old lady's heart. By the time she left, after a guided tour of the castle and a delicious tea, she was convinced that Lady Elizabeth was 'the one girl who could make Bertie happy'.

Drastic action was now needed. The mothers put their heads together and it was decided that it was time for James to go away for a while. So in the early days of 1922, he was dispatched to the oil fields of Oklahoma to be a rigger. By the time he returned, Lady Elizabeth had married Bertie and become the Duchess of York. In any case Lady Strathmore had decided that he was not a suitable match for her youngest daughter, given his wild ways and his broken engagement. He had no money of his own and nor had she, being the ninth child and fourth daughter of an Earl still up to his ears in debt. Although greatly distinguished later in life, at that stage James showed no signs of earning a living. As he was fond of saying himself, 'There is no point in marrying for love for love does not last but money does.' Instead he married where money was, Lady Rachel Cavendish, the fourth daughter of the Duke of Devonshire, on Elizabeth's twenty-third birthday, 4 August 1923. A solicitor drew up the marriage contract and according to the jilted Elfie's daughter, Lady Rachel proved to be just the sort of wife he wanted. 'She was beautiful, she was rich, and she was the most marvellously loyal and tolerant wife that any philanderer could have hoped to have.' Moreover, Lady Elizabeth had got his measure. She had noticed his roving eye during the Ascot race meeting of 1921 and considered him, for all his charm, unsuitable husband material.

The way was now clear for Bertie and he pursued Lady Elizabeth with the same persistent obstinacy that had seen him through so many troubles earlier in his life. In February his sister, Princess Mary, married Viscount Lascelles and Lady Elizabeth was one of the bridesmaids. Intimate dinner parties followed at the home of the Hon Mrs Greville and the shooting season again found Bertie at Glamis. This time 'Chips' Channon was also among the house party. As he records in his diary, 'One rainy afternoon, we were sitting about and I pretended I could read cards, and I told Elizabeth Lyon's fortune and predicted a great and

46

glamorous royal future. She laughed, for it was obvious that the Duke of York was much in love with her.' After the visit, Bertie wrote to his mother, 'The more I see of her, the more I like her.'

On 5 January 1923 the *Daily News* thought they had a scoop when they erroneously announced in banner headlines 'A Scottish Bride for the Prince of Wales . . . An Official Announcement Imminent.' Bertie was furious and issued a denial. Down at Firle, staying with Lord Gage, Lady Elizabeth was teased. As 'Chips' Channon reported, 'The evening papers have announced her engagement to the Prince of Wales. So we all bowed and bobbed and teased her, calling her "Ma'am": I am not sure that she enjoyed it. It couldn't be true, but how delighted everyone would be! She certainly has something on her mind. She is more gentle, lovely and exquisite than any woman alive, but this evening I thought her unhappy and *distraite*. I longed to tell her I would die for her, although I am not in love with her.'

Eight days later, at her Hertfordshire home, St Paul's Walden Bury, Lady Elizabeth and Prince Albert skipped church and went for a walk in the woods. Bertie proposed again and this time she accepted. His delighted parents received the telegram they had so long awaited. It simply said, 'All right Bertie.'

The official announcement two days later surprised 'Chips' Channon, among others. 'I was so startled and almost fell out of bed when I read the Court Circular. We have all hoped, waited, so long for this romance to prosper, that we had begun to despair that she would ever accept him ... He is the luckiest of men, and there is not a man in England today who doesn't envy him. The clubs are in gloom.'

The wedding was set for 26 April and an engagement ring of a sapphire flanked by two diamonds was specially made. Lady Elizabeth based herself at the family's new London house, 17

Bruton Street, as congratulations and presents poured in. She admitted to friends feeling very happy but 'loathed' the press attention. Perhaps to silence them, she innocently gave her one and only newspaper interview. A gentle admonition came from the Palace and the mistake was never repeated. The King and Queen were delighted with her. 'Elizabeth is with us now, so well brought up, a great addition to the family,' wrote Bertie's mother approvingly.

The Queen gave her a diamond and sapphire necklace as a wedding present while the King chose a tiara and complete ensemble of diamonds and turquoises. From her father she received a diamond tiara and a necklace of pearls and diamonds. Bertie gave her a necklace of diamonds and pearls and she in turn gave him a dress watch chain of platinum and pearls.

No less precious was a gift from her own troupe of Girl Guides at Glamis, a silver pen and ink stand. The people of

Forfar wrote to ask what gift would be appropriate. She replied with her natural sensitivity that, given 'everyone is feeling the pinch', she would treasure an illuminated address. No money, she insisted, was to be spent in these times of hardship.

On the morning of her wedding, flanked by Lord Strathmore, she travelled in a state landau to Westminster Abbey, the first royal bride to be married there since 1382, when King Richard II took Princess Anne of Bohemia for his wife. Elizabeth's dress was medieval in style, of machine-made Nottingham lace with a veil of Flanders lace, lent by Queen Mary. The groom wore the uniform of a Group Captain of the Royal Air Force. In a spontaneous gesture, as she entered the Abbey, Lady Elizabeth placed her bouquet of York roses and white heather on the tomb of the Unknown Soldier. Her beloved brother Fergus, who had fallen so bravely in the service of his country, was not to be forgotten even on this most special of days. All other royal brides have chosen to follow her example although they now keep their bouquet until they are on their way back from the altar. A request that some of the ceremony might be broadcast on the wireless was rejected on the grounds that 'disrespectful people might hear the service, perhaps even some of them sitting in public houses with their hats on.'

After the wedding breakfast at Buckingham Palace, where they faced the daunting task of cutting the nine-feet-high cake, the newlyweds left on honeymoon, first to Polesden Lacey in Surrey, the home of a mutual friend, and later to Glamis. Unfortunately the weather in Scotland was so bad that the new Duchess of York went down with whooping cough, which she later described as 'not a very romantic disease.'

If Elizabeth had had her doubts about the marriage, they were to prove unfounded. As the wise Lady Airlie had predicted, love grew apace as the list of their official engagements mounted. The new Duchess's confidence in public rubbed off on her husband and he was further helped by the Australian speech therapist, Lionel Logue, who taught him a new way of breathing to correct his stammer.

When he had to make a speech, he now had the Duchess at his side mouthing the words he had to say and occasionally touching his hand for reassurance. As Bertie wrote from Balmoral to Mr Logue, he could even get his father to understand him. 'Up here I have been talking a lot with the King, and I have no trouble at all. Also, I can make him listen and I don't have to repeat everything over again.' In private, the Duchess used to try to make life as serene for him as possible. On evenings off, a supper tray would be sent up to the private sitting-room they shared and if the Duke was away from home, she wrote to him every day.

The Duchess even found a way of

deflecting his nervous rages, known in the family as 'gnashes'. She would gently take his pulse and count, 'tick, tick, tick, one, two, three', which invariably made him smile. The normal cause of these upsets was her chronic unpunctuality, Like Bertie's grandmother, Queen Alexandra, who nearly missed her own Coronation because she was so late, 'the dear little Duchess' as she was known, could not turn up on time. It was not unusual to find Bertie pacing up and down the corridor, muttering, 'Where *is* that damned woman?' She was even late for dinner with her father-in-law, something no one else would have dared to be. As the Duke cringed behind her, expecting an almighty blast from his father, his wife laughingly apologized. To everyone's astonishment, the King merely replied, 'Not at all, my dear. You are not late. I think we must have sat down a few minutes early.'

Elizabeth had no difficulty in getting on well with the King. She realized early on that his bark was worse than his bite and she became deeply fond of him. As she wrote to the royal physician after his death in 1936, 'I miss him dreadfully.Unlike his own children I was never afraid of him, and in all the twelve years of having me as a daughter-in-law, he never spoke one unkind or abrupt word to me, and was always ready to listen and give advice on one's own silly little affairs. He was so kind and *dependable*! And when he was in a mood, he could be deliciously funny too!'

The couple's happiness was plain for all to see. As the diplomat Duff Cooper wrote to his wife after going to the theatre with them, 'The Duke and Duchess of York were there. They are such a sweet little couple and so fond of one another. They reminded me of us, sitting together in the box having private jokes, and in the interval when we were all sitting in the room behind the box they slipped out, and I found them standing together in a dark corner of the passage talking happily as we might. She affects no shadow of airs and graces.'

Their first home, when they returned to London from their honeymoon, was White Lodge in Richmond Park, formerly the home of Queen Mary and now the headquarters of the Royal Ballet School. It was large, cold, damp and ugly. The Duchess wrote to her mother begging her to send down some of her personal possessions from Glamis to make the place more homely. Despite having her belongings about her, the Duchess was frequently ill during the next year which greatly worried her husband. A bad bout of bronchitis doubled his anxiety and he was determined that his delicate bride would not endure another English winter. He arranged for a safari to East Africa over Christmas 1924. The trip lasted four months and they both returned to Britain rested and healthy. In August they left for Glamis and Balmoral, and to everyone's delight, the

Duchess announced that she was expecting their first child.

On 19 November, an urgent message arrived from Sandringham to say that Queen Alexandra, the Queen Mother, had suffered a severe heart attack. During their bleak childhood, their grandmother had been their one source of affection and warmth, and David and Bertie hurried to her bedside. Unfortunately, fog came down over East Anglia and by the time they arrived, the house was in darkness. They had lost their race to say goodbye. Queen Alexandra was dead.

On Wednesday, 21 April 1926, Elizabeth Alexandra Mary was born at twenty minutes to three in the morning at the Strathmore's London home, 17 Bruton Street. It was a difficult birth and a Caesarean section was necessary. The King and Queen hurried up from Windsor to see their baby granddaughter. Queen Mary noted that the new princess was 'a little darling with a lovely complexion and fair hair.'

The christening took place in the private chapel at Buckingham Palace on 29 May and the baby was blessed with holy water from the River Jordan. 'Of course poor baby cried,' the Queen wrote in her diary. Apparently the efforts of her grandmother, her mother and the Archbishop of York failed to still the child and it was only after she was handed back to her nurse, the Duchess's faithful old nanny Allah, that she was quietened. The solution, said the Press, lay in a bottle.

Their happiness now complete, the Duke and Duchess settled down to family life and found themselves a permanent home at 145 Piccadilly. However, they were not to enjoy their peace for long. When Lilibet, as the little Princess was nicknamed, was just eight months old, the royal couple were asked by the King to undertake a six-month tour of Australia and New Zealand. Despite the Duchess falling ill with tonsillitis during the early part of the trip, the tour was most definitely a triumph. As the Duke happily wrote to his father, 'I had to make three speeches the first morning . . . I had perfect confidence in myself and did not hesitate at all.'

Queen Mary took charge of the nursery and Allah and the Princess moved to Buckingham Palace. The Queen's cousin, Lady Mary Clayton, then aged nine, remembers afternoons there. 'Luckily my governess and Allah were great friends and I used to be taken to Buckingham Palace to play with my cousin. I had always longed for a baby sister and she was absolutely sweet—delicious. If it was fine we used to play in the gardens and, if not, we would be round the fire playing games.'

She says Lilibet was a very good-humoured child and, as she grew older, would always 'listen to reason'. 'Occasionally she wouldn't answer but that was only because she was [pretending to be] a horse and couldn't.' However, there was one problem. Lilibet kept overhearing other nannies saying, "Oh! You can't tell her off. She's a Princess" and this led her to believe that she could do no wrong,' recalls Lady Mary. 'One day we were playing cards with my mother and Lilibet was cheating. When she was told off, she replied, "I can cheat if I want to, I'm a Princess." Well, we all started cheating and she saw that it was pointless to play a game if you cheated. And she never did it again.'

Meanwhile, Lilibet's parents busied themselves with an ever-increasing round of public duties; the Duke was heavily involved with everything from the Industrial Welfare Society to Dr Barnado's Homes while the Duchess concentrated on hospitals, child welfare and needlework. Whenever possible, they liked to carry out engagements together. August 1930 found the royal couple as usual ensconced at Glamis and on the twenty-first, as thunder and lightning rattled round the castle battlements, Princess Margaret Rose was born at twenty-two minutes past nine in the evening. Again it was a Caesarean birth. There was much rejoicing and a huge bonfire on Hunter's Hill, despite the downpour, because she was the first royal baby born north of the border since 1602. The Duchess had wanted to call her second daughter Margaret Anne, but the latter name was vetoed by the King. Lilibet instantly christened her younger sister 'Bud' explaining that she was not yet full grown.

Lady Mary recalls the young Margaret Rose well. 'She was quite unlike her sister. She was the naughty one—full of mischief, a real monkey but a charming one. She was always up to some prank. I remember once, she nearly drowned one of the royal detectives. He was bending down trying to get something out of the lake, when she leapt onto his shoulders forcing him under-water. I can see her now, sitting on his shoulders laughing her head off while we all tried to pull her off.'

And so the happy, tranquil years

unfolded. The Duke and Duchess acquired Royal Lodge in Windsor Great Park as their country retreat and, with the help of their daughters, created a wonderful garden. A little Welsh cottage, given to Princess Elizabeth on her sixth birthday, was built in the grounds and there were ponies and pets. The girls were frequent visitors to Glamis where they played the popular games of the day, including the rather dangerous practice of putting ha'pennies on the railway track so the oncoming train could flatten them into pennies.

On 15 January 1936, King George V, now in his seventy-first year, caught a chill while staying at Sandringham and took to his bed. The young Princesses were staying with their grandparents while their mother recovered from pneumonia and took advantage of the winter weather to make a snowman and have a snowball fight. Hearing their laughter, the King looked out of the window to watch the fun. Later that day, the princesses were on their way home after saying goodbye to Grandpapa. They were aged just nine and five. Two days later, at five minutes to midnight on 20 January, as Queen Mary read aloud to him in the flickering firelight, King George V passed away. David was proclaimed King Edward VIII.

The Duchess of York had never liked the racy set. She hated her sister-in-law, Dorothy, married to her oldest brother, Patrick, Lord Glamis, because she smoked and drank cocktails. Therefore neither she nor Bertie, who was of the same mind, had much in common with the Fort Belvedere set who surrounded the new King and, although living close by, they were infrequent guests.

The Yorks particularly disliked the King's latest companion, Wallis Simpson, whom they had met two years before at a reception held to honour the wedding of the Duke of Kent. As her close friend Helen Hardinge recalled. 'I am afraid Mrs Simpson went down badly with the Duchess from the word go . . . The Duchess of York was never discourteous in my experience, but those of us who knew her very well could always tell when she did not care for something or someone, and it was very apparent to me that she did not care for Mrs Simpson at all.'

To make matters worse, Wallis, sensing her disapproval, took to making fun of her and dubbed her 'the Dowdy Duchess'. She was fond of mimicking her goody-goodiness which she claimed was false and artificial. On one such occasion she was caught in mid-act when the Duchess walked unexpectedly into the room. Even the young princesses' governess, Marion Crawford, did not like the look of Wallis when she visited the family at Royal Lodge. 'She was a smart, attractive woman, already middle-aged, but with that immediate friendliness American women have. She appeared to be entirely at her ease; if anything, rather too much so.'

'Chips' Channon reported that the

King was 'insane' about the twice-divorced American and rumours circulated that her hold over him was due to expert sexual techniques she had learnt while on a visit to China. However, some biographers have suggested that the bout of mumps he endured during his time at Dartmouth rendered him virtually impotent, and that one of the reasons why he gave up the throne was the knowledge that he would not be able to produce an heir.

For his summer holiday in 1936 the King chartered a yacht, and Mrs Simpson and a group of friends joined him for a cruise on the Dalmatian coast. Photographs of them cavorting in the sunshine were in stark contrast to the staid family holiday of the Duke and Duchess of York in Scotland. In September the King joined them and asked if they could take on one of his public engagements, opening Aberdeen Royal Infirmary, because he was snowed under with work. They duly opened the hospital but while they were so doing the King was spotted at Ballater railway station awaiting the arrival of Mrs Simpson. As 'Chips' Channon reported. 'The visit to Balmoral was a calamity, after the King chucked opening the Aberdeen Infirmary, and then openly appeared at Ballater station on the same day to welcome Wallis to the Highlands. Aberdeen will never forgive him.' The incident was not reported in the British press, which discreetly avoided printing any reference to Mrs Simpson.

On 27 October, Wallis received her decree nisi from Ernest Simpson and would soon be free to marry. The American press went wild and speculation was rife that she would become Edward's Queen Consort. The King knew this to be impossible and suggested a morganatic marriage, whereby any children of the union do not inherit, to the Prime Minister Stanley Baldwin. This was rejected outright by the self-governing countries of the Empire and the King announced his intention to abdicate. Shocked and hurt, Queen Mary wrote to him. 'It seemed inconceivable to those who had made such a sacrifice during the war that you, as their King, refused a lesser sacrifice. After all, all my life I have put my country before everything else, and I simply cannot change now.'

The Queen was later to describe Bertie as 'appalled' by the idea of kingship. She told her biographer Harold Nicolson, 'He was devoted to his brother and the whole abdication crisis made him miserable. He sobbed on my shoulder for a whole hour—there, upon that sofa.' In her typically understated way, she was later to describe the abdication crisis as 'a pretty kettle of fish'.

As the Duchess of York read her Bible on 10 December 1936, her husband and his younger brothers witnessed the King signing the instrument of abdication. The document was read to both houses of Parliament the next day and duly passed. That evening the departing King broadcast to the nation. He told his people that 'I have found it impossible to carry the heavy burden of responsibility and discharge my duties as King as I would wish to do without the help and support of the woman I love.' He added that the Duke of York had 'one matchless blessing, enjoyed by so many of you and not bestowed on me, a happy home with his wife and children.' The day after her accession, the new Queen-Empress Elizabeth was able to write, 'I can hardly now believe that we have been called to this tremendous task and ... the curious thing is that we are not afraid. I feel God has enabled us to face the situation calmly.'

Certainly one person would have been pleased, the late King George V, who had always had a fondness for Elizabeth. He had remarked of his children that 'Bertie has more guts than the rest of them put together' and in the last weeks of his life, he exclaimed passionately, after being reminded yet again of David's liaison with Wallis, 'I pray to God that my eldest son will never marry and have children, and that nothing will come between Bertie and Lilibet and the throne.' Little could he have known then that it would not be long before his wish was granted.

CHAPTER THREE

QUEEN AND COUNTRY

Baron Charteris of Amisfield, the Queen's private secretary for twenty-seven years, has commented that the key to the Queen Mother's success was her zest for life. 'It was her totally positive attitude which helped to re-establish respect for the monarchy after the catastrophe of the abdication of her brother-in-law, King Edward VIII.'

Another former courtier goes further: 'There would have been no Royal Family today if it had not been for her,' he says. 'George VI was painfully shy and had a dreadful stammer. He desperately did not want to be King, believing he was utterly unsuited. Without Elizabeth, he would probably have gone to pieces.'

After the terrible days of the Abdication crisis, Bertie was angry, tired out, astonished, bewildered, and to a certain extent, bitter. His speech impediment, which had eased so dramatically in the quiet, contented years with Elizabeth, reappeared with a vengeance. To make matters worse, the Royal Family itself was said to be split and strange stories were told about the last hours before Edward VIII finally abdicated. He was labelled 'the rubber-stamp' King, who was so weak that he would go along with whatever he was told. It was hinted that Edward VIII had really gone because he had stood up to the politicians, criticizing their support of people in depressed areas, following the National Strike and the Yarrow March. Now it was suggested that the Establishment had secured themselves a 'Yes' man.

After weeks of stress, Elizabeth collapsed with an attack of flu. Queen Mary went to see her and the faithful but indiscreet governess Miss Marion Crawford, who was waiting at the door, reported, 'Queen Mary came out of the door and tears were streaming down her face. The Duchess was lying propped up among pillows. I thought that she too had been crying. She held out her hand to me. "I'm afraid there are going to be some great changes in our lives, Crawfie. We must take what is coming to us and make the best of it." '

The Prime Minister, Stanley Baldwin, had no illusions about the former King. He told the biographer Harold Nicolson: 'You see, Nicolson, the man is mad. *Mad* . . . he could see nothing but that woman. He did not realize that any other considerations avail. He lacks religion . . . He doesn't realize that there is anything beyond. I told his mother so.'

Mrs Keppel, his grandfather, King Edward VII's mistress, commented 'the King has shown neither decency, nor wisdom, nor regard for tradition' and his private secretary summed him up thus, 'He was without soul and this made him a trifle mad . . . He never cared for England or the English . . . He rather hated this country . . . and did not like being reminded of his duties.'

This was to be the new Queen's finest hour. She stood foursquare behind her husband and, although upset and exhausted herself, used all her courage and guile to soothe, encourage and bolster the King. She fulfilled the promise he had made on the day of his accession. 'With my wife and helpmate by my side, I take up the heavy task which lies before me.' Only her obstinate support could persuade him that he was capable and worthy of assuming the mantle of the monarchy.

Bertie proved his gratitude on his birthday, 14 December, three days after David had left Britain, when he gave his wife the highest honour in his gift, the Order of the Garter. The Queen was touched and wrote tactfully to her mother-in-law, Queen Mary, 'He had discovered that Papa gave it to you, on his, Papa's birthday, and the coincidence was so charming that he has now followed suit and given it to me on his own birthday.' Naturally it was much more than that.

Now Bertie was settled, it was time to turn her attention to her daughters, Princess Elizabeth, aged ten, and Margaret Rose, six. There was to be an unwelcome sea change in their lives and she was determined that they would hear it from her and her alone. She had been so preoccupied and so busy in the preceding days that she initially had a discreet conference with their governess to find out what they knew. Then taking Margaret on her knee and seating Princess Elizabeth beside her, she quietly explained what had happened, the changes to come and the new responsibilities they faced. The idea of living at Buckingham Palace did not appeal to the future Queen. 'You mean for *ever*?' she asked her mother incredulously and suggested that an underground passage be dug across Green Park so she could sleep in her own bed. The Coronation of Edward VIII had been set for 12 May 1937, and after the Abdication, the Prime

Minister, Stanley Baldwin, asked Parliament if it should be postponed. 'Same day. New King,' came the reply. So the Coronation was to go ahead as planned.

After a brief respite at Sandringham, when the happy news of the birth of Princess Alexandra of Kent, daughter of the Duke and Duchess of Kent, on Christmas Day lifted their spirits, Queen Elizabeth faced one of the busiest periods of her life. Not only had she and the family to move house but she had to learn the procedure of the Coronation and order her clothes for the ceremony. Her dress was made by Handley Seymour and at a long table at the Royal School of Needlework in Kensington, ten women sat embroidering the emblems of all parts of the British Empire upon the robe. A young designer named Norman Hartnell made the dresses for her Maids of Honour. Soon he was to replace Mr Seymour as the Queen's favourite couturier.

Meanwhile the King was struggling with the monarch's red boxes, containing all the papers of State. Having never been trained in the routine duties of the sovereign, he was horrified by the amount of work that he had to get through and his meticulous eye for detail meant he spent far longer over his papers than most. Like his great-grandfather, Prince Albert, who worked himself to an early grave, he found that if things were to be done to his satisfaction, he needed to rise early and go to bed late. The Queen worried about his health and made his brief spells at home as quiet and undisturbed as possible. In addition, there was the heavy programme of official engagements, so essential to restore public confidence after the Abdication. The King and Queen picked the East End of London for their first state drive, on 13 February, and to their relief received a rousing reception at the People's Palace, a popular entertainment hall in Mile End Road.

The victory of the horse Royal Mail and their presence at Aintree made the Grand National a red-letter day. At Wembley, Sunderland beat Preston North End in the FA Championship and the victorious captain received the cup and congratulations from Queen Elizabeth.

To add to the excitement, Service contingents began arriving from overseas; first the Australians, then the New Zealanders, followed by the Royal Canadian Mounted Police and hand-picked men from the regiments of India and Burma. Great electric chandeliers were hoisted into position at Westminster Abbey as the Queen took her part in rehearsals and the King worked hard with his speech therapist, Mr Logue, so that he would be word perfect on the big day.

Kings and Chiefs, Presidents and Premiers arrived daily, lions and crowns were gilded, flag poles were erected and a wide red carpet was unrolled along the Abbey's nave. The King and Queen were awoken from their sleep at three o'clock on the morning of their Coronation by a technician testing the loud speakers on Constitution Hill; the tramp of soldiers taking up their positions along the Mall coupled with the exuberant festivities of the crowds who had camped overnight made further rest impossible.

It was to be a long, triumphant and historic day. Precedent would be broken in two ways; the ceremony would be broadcast and that stickler for tradition, the Queen Dowager, Queen Mary, would overcome her prejudices and attend the crowning of her late husband's successor. Also, more than five million people would pour into the capital to cheer their King and Queen. The tide was beginning to turn in their favour but the royal couple were not yet home and dry.

The Princesses, despite fears that Margaret Rose might fall asleep, witnessed the ceremony, which lasted three hours and forty minutes, under the watchful eye of their grandmother, Queen Mary, and their aunt, the Princess Royal. Princess Elizabeth had asserted that it 'would be a disgrace to us all' should somnolence overtake her sister and kept her amused with books and whispered confidences.

Both King George VI and Queen Elizabeth found the ceremony very moving. As the Duchess of Devonshire remarked, 'The Queen is a person of real piety, who felt her crowning acutely.' The Archbishop of Canterbury, Dr Lang, wrote of their spiritual preparation for the event. 'After some talk on the spiritual significance of the Coronation, they knelt with me; I prayed for them and for the realm and Empire, and I gave them my personal blessing. I was much moved, and so were they. Indeed, there were tears in their eyes when we rose from our knees.'

Bertie had chosen the name of George in a public attempt to emulate his father George V, who had been such a dependable and popular monarch. In his Coronation broadcast, the new King pledged, 'The Queen and I will always keep in our hearts the inspiration of this day. May we ever be worthy of the good will, which I am proud to think, surrounds us at the outset of my reign. I thank you from my heart, and may God bless you all.' However, whatever name he chose, the Prime Minister was only too aware that the new King and his Consort had a very difficult task ahead of them. There were many who felt that his older brother should not have been denied the throne for the sake of love, and a sentimental sympathy for David swept the land.

The British press, who had kept so loyally silent during much of the Wallis affair, were now in full cry. They criticized the King's poor academic record at naval college, which some even suggested made him unfit to reign. Unflattering comparisons were made between the two brothers; David was portrayed as charming and of the people. Bertie was perceived as awkward, aloof and lacking in 'presence'. His stammer was frequently mentioned as a disadvantage.

Stanley Baldwin told the faithful Mabell, Countess of Airlie, that he felt the new King was beginning his reign with a lot of prejudice against him. 'He's had no chance to capture the popular imagination as his brother did. I'm afraid he won't find it easy going for the first year or two.' Lady Airlie was more concerned for her old friend Elizabeth. 'I pitied most of all the new Queen. In the fourteen years of her marriage she had remained completely unspoiled, still at heart the simple unaffected girl I had known at Glamis, carrying out her public duties with an efficiency that won Queen Mary's admiration, but finding her true happiness in her home and her own family circle.' Queen Mary, however, was more optimistic than her lady-in-waiting. 'The Yorks will do it very well,' she confidently predicted.

And they did. In July the King and

Queen visited Edinburgh and the crowds turned out to cheer them. The Queen was invested with the Order of the Thistle at St Giles Cathedral, the first and only lady to receive that honour. The King had surprised his Consort on the evening of his Coronation by presenting her with a beautiful diamond badge and star to be worn at her investiture.

Meanwhile the Duke of Windsor had married Wallis Simpson at the Château de Cande in France. To the former King's anger and sadness, no member of the Royal Family attended the wedding on 3 June and his wife was debarred from using the title Her Royal Highness. The wound was never healed and was still open thirty-five years later when the Duke of Windsor died in 1972.

Society too turned its back on the Windsors and many of their friends pretended never to have known them. Despite protestations, the greatest party-giver of them all, Emerald Cunard, was never again to enjoy royal favour. Almost the only exceptions were Duff and Lady Diana Cooper, who had been frequent guests at Fort Belvedere. They were invited to Windsor Castle for the weekend and the Queen sat up late drinking tea with the diplomat. 'She put her feet up on a sofa and talked of Kingship and "the intolerable honour" but not of the crisis', he recalled. His wife commented how different was the new regime compared to the old days of Edward VIII. 'That was an operetta,' she said. 'This is an institution.' The press and the public agreed and by the end of 1937 the popularity of King George VI and his Queen was firmly established. They attracted huge crowds wherever they went and Queen Elizabeth endeared herself to the people. Ever mischievous, she once even lobbed one of her caramels through the royal car's open window to an onlooking policeman.

However, there were more troubles on the way as it became increasingly apparent that war was brewing in

Europe. In March 1938, Hitler's army invaded Austria and weeks later, Czechoslovakia was at risk as the Chancellor backed a rebellion by Germans in the Sudetenland. Soon, Hitler was to announce that the country no longer existed. As the crisis intensified, it was decided that the King and Queen should visit the allies—France, Canada and the United States.

Shortly before the first of these visits, the Queen's mother, Lady Strathmore, died at the age of seventy-five. The tour was postponed for three weeks and her daughter, valiant as ever, 'captured Paris by storm' in her white mourning dresses—a *tour de force* by designer Sir Norman Hartnell. In Canada, the royal couple were welcomed by crowds estimated at over half a million and in Washington they received a tumultuous reception. One Texan member of the House of Representatives declared, 'Cousin Elizabeth, you're a thousand times more pretty than your pictures.'

Their duty very well done, the family

travelled to Balmoral in August where the King held his annual boys' camp at Abergeldy Castle, a few miles away. As the Royal Family joined in a singsong, Hitler was preparing to invade Poland. The King returned to London with the Queen close on his heels. Within two weeks. Britain was at war and the young men of the King's camp were joining the services. It was said the Queen was 'a tower of strength' and she in turn took strength from her faith, recalling the Bowes Lyon family motto 'In thou, my God, I place my trust without changes to the end.' It had seen her through difficult times before and would do so again.

At Buckingham Palace, staff immediately rejoined their regiments and a Home Guard was formed among those who remained. It was decided that the Princesses should be evacuated to Windsor but the King and Queen steadfastly refused to leave London, even during the Blitz. As the 'few' fought over the skies in the Battle of

Britain in 1940 and invasion seemed imminent, it was suggested that Elizabeth and Margaret Rose be sent to Canada but the Queen was having none of it. 'The Princesses will never leave without me. I will not leave without the King—and the King will never leave,' she asserted. During the worst of the bombing, they visited the East End of London to witness for themselves the carnage and destruction. As one of the women wrote to Dame Barbara Cartland, herself very active during the war, 'The Queen came down yesterday morning—God bless her. She was so kind and she said to me: "I am so sorry for you. I know what you are feeling." The way she spoke was like the voice of an angel. Though I hadn't shed a tear over my home in ruins, and my little dog dead, I cried like a baby. There's never been a lady like her—and that's the truth.'

The Queen wrote to her mother-in-law, Queen Mary, 'I feel quite exhausted after seeing and hearing so much sadness, sorrow, heroism and magnificent spirit. The destruction is so awful and the people are so wonderful—they deserve a better world.' When Buckingham Palace was hit, she remarked, 'I'm glad we've been bombed. It makes me feel I can look the East End in the face.' The Palace was bombed nine times in all and the Guards Chapel, nearby, was completely destroyed killing over 100 worshippers.

Mr Chris Friend, Pearly King of the Isle of Dogs and Poplar, remembers her visits well. 'I was about thirteen at the time and it is a day I will never forget. The streets were full of rubble. People were living in terrible conditions. Families were living on the pavement or in the basements of the bombed-out buildings. As she picked her way through the destruction, she had a word for everybody. People couldn't believe it. She just came and chatted as if she had known them all her life. She was in the same predicament and it was a real morale booster to the whole of the East

End. My mother and her friends were in tears, something I had never seen before and was never to see again. She was fabulous. We never forgot her and she never forgot us. As far as we were concerned she was the greatest royal favourite there has ever been, and she would always be Number One.' And the people of the East End have been as good as their word. Every year, on her birthday, a huge cake is delivered with the compliments of those she comforted through the bad times they all endured.

It was to be the same throughout Britain. The King and Queen travelled the length and breadth of the nation on the royal train giving sympathy and support. Hardly a battle station, factory or farm was ignored as they comforted the homeless and bereaved and spurred on the troops. It might have been Churchill's finest hour but it was theirs too. While the former King had visited Berlin just before the war and allied himself with the Fascists, the British people rejected Nazism in all its seductive guises and with it, David, Edward VIII. Despite many requests to be involved and allowed to return to the country in a time of crisis, the Duke was kept safely out of the way as Governor of the Bahamas.

On 25 August 1942, the Duke of Kent left Balmoral Castle, after spending a few days with the King and Queen, to fly to Iceland where he was due to inspect RAF bases. But his plane crashed in the Scottish mountains and he was killed. The King, who had been very close to his younger brother, was devastated. A year earlier, the Queen's nephew, John, Lord Glamis, had been killed in action, so the Royal Family not only shared in the personal bereavement of their people but also the privations of war. As the American President's wife, Eleanor Roosevelt, noted when she visited in 1942, rationing was as strict at the Palace as it was elsewhere. 'We were served on gold and silver plates, but our bread was the same kind of war bread every other family had to eat ... nothing was ever served that was not served in any war canteen.'

Green lines were painted on baths to ensure that no one was tempted to use too much hot water; the magnificent gardens at Royal Lodge were dug up and turned over to vegetables, tended by the Princesses; and shooting ranges were constructed both at Buckingham Palace and Windsor. Every morning the Queen received instruction in how to fire a revolver, declaring, 'I shall not go down like the others.' To help, Churchill sent her an automatic weapon of great efficiency.

The Royal Family were also anxious to make sure that they contributed to the war effort in a personal way. The Queen and her staff made bandages and dressings for the Red Cross, while the King spent two evenings a week making ammunition. Princess Elizabeth was also keen to do her bit and plagued her father to be allowed to join one of the women's services as soon as she passed her sixteenth birthday. The King thought her too young but was finally persuaded by the Queen and in March 1945, she entered the records of the Auxiliary Territorial Service as No. 230873 Second Subaltern Elizabeth Alexandra Mary Windsor. The princess learnt how to drive and to change the wheels on a lorry and as the Queen told one of her senior officers. 'Last night we had sparking plugs during the whole of dinner!'

Although the Queen was strict as far as her daughters' education was concerned, she also made sure that they had their fair share of fun. She arranged birthday parties and dances at the castle and invited young Guards officers, stationed at depots nearby. These were highly informal affairs of the 'knees up' variety with games and music after supper. It became routine for the King and Queen to lead congas round the ballroom.

Meanwhile, in Princess Elizabeth's room was a photograph of a handsome young naval officer. Letters were passing between Prince Philip and herself, and during his leaves they met on a number of occasions. They danced at a party given by the Duchess of Kent and, at Christmas 1943, he was among the guests invited to Windsor. As usual there was the annual pantomime; Elizabeth played Aladdin and Margaret Rose, the Princess. Elizabeth is said to have given a particularly sparkling performance as the young Lieutenant watched from the front row. 'Philip thinks this' and 'Philip thinks that' began to pepper her daily conversation.

On 8 May 1945, the unconditional surrender of Germany was announced and the war was over in Europe. The crowds surged up the Mall to cheer the King and Queen, who were flanked by their daughters and Sir Winston Churchill, as they stood on the balcony of Buckingham Palace. Amid scenes of wild jubilation, the VE Day celebrations continued far into the night and the Princesses asked if they might join the revellers. 'Poor darlings', said the King, 'they've never had any fun yet' and permission was given on condition that they were escorted by a small party of male friends.

The girls slipped out of a side entrance and, unrecognized, joined the throng as they cheered their parents. Then, going with the tide of the crowd, they were swept along the Mall and Whitehall before ending up doing the conga through all the best hotels in town. During their two-hour foray, Princess Margaret stole a sailor's hat and the unfortunate man chased her all the way back to the Palace, never realizing who she was. Our present Queen was to say of the outing, 'I think it was one of the most memorable moments of my life.'

It was said of Lady Strathmore that she had 'a genius for family life' and it was a trait her youngest daughter inherited. Teatime became a focal point in the life of the Royal Family when they all gathered together round the fire to discuss the events of the day and any problems that had arisen. One topic that came up increasingly frequently was Princess Elizabeth's cousin, Lieutenant Philip Mountbatten. The pair had fallen in love during the war years and now wished to announce their engagement at Christmas 1946. However, the King and Queen thought otherwise, and wished there to be a pause to make sure the couple were certain of their feelings. So both Princesses joined their parents on a four-month tour of South Africa in the New Year of 1947, with a certain Group Captain Peter Townsend going as their equerry. While Princess Elizabeth pined for her sweetheart, a friendship between her younger sister, Princess Margaret Rose, then sixteen, and the Group Captain began. Little did they know it was to cause them both heartache.

On 9 July, Princess Elizabeth and Prince Philip announced their engagement and the Princess proudly showed off her platinum and diamond ring at the garden party that afternoon. The marriage took place at Westminster Abbey on 20 November, the first great State occasion since the war and the huge crowds were determined to enjoy themselves despite the times of austerity. The King wrote to his newly married daughter, 'I was so proud of you and thrilled at having you so close to me on our long walk in Westminster Abbey, but when I handed your hand to the Archbishop I felt I had lost something very precious.'

Princess Margaret, however, was still at home and was the apple of the King's eye. 'He adored both his daughters,' recalls a courtier, 'but Margaret, he spoilt.' With her quick wit, she could make him laugh even when he was angry with her and she got away with murder. Once, when she was asked by her parents not to be so free with the sherry, she replied firmly that she would launch no more ships unless her glass was refilled. When she was questioned about her use of modern slang, she joked that she had learnt it, 'At my mother's knee, or some such low joint.'

She was 'Papa's girl' and they loved to have fun together. When he was not very well or feeling rather low, she would sing funny songs to amuse him and would mimic mutual friends. Charades was another favourite entertainment and it was not unknown for the King to don a false moustache and a cardboard policeman's helmet from a cracker to add to the fun. But soon there were to be fewer parties as the King's health deteriorated. When Prince Charles was born on 14 November 1948, his grandfather was lying ill under the same roof. Doctors were called to investigate cramp in his legs and they discovered hardening of the arteries which later necessitated an operation. The Queen and Princess Elizabeth took on an increasing load of official duties as the King was ordered to rest. Shortly after the birth of Princess Anne on 15 August 1950, he was found to have cancer and had to have a lung removed. Princess Elizabeth rang every day from Canada, fearing she might never see her father again.

In December 1951, the King was well enough to pre-record his Christmas broadcast and went, as usual, to Sandringham for the New Year. He told his family that he felt so much better that he was happy to send Princess Elizabeth and the Duke of Edinburgh away on a five-month tour of Australia and New Zealand, visiting Kenya on the way. On the eve of their departure, the whole family spent an evening at the Theatre Royal, Drury Lane, enjoying the première of the musical *South Pacific*. Despite the bitter cold of a late January day, the King stood bareheaded on the tarmac to wave his daughter goodbye, not returning into the warmth of the Heathrow terminal until the last speck of her aeroplane had disappeared. A week later, on 6 February, the King died in his sleep, aged fifty-six, at Sandringham after enjoying a good day's shooting.

The new Queen heard the news after spending the night in a tree-house in Kenya watching big game. She returned immediately to London, wearing the black mourning clothes packed in her travelling wardrobes—just in case. As the light was fading, she stepped on to British soil, and a letter was handed to her in her mother's hand. 'Her old Grannie and subject must be the first to kiss her hand.' At half past four Queen Mary drove from Marlborough House to Clarence House to pay obedience to the new monarch, the seventh she had known, Queen Elizabeth, the new Queen Mother, faced widowhood at the age of fifty-one.

The Duke and Duchess of Windsor had received the news of the King's death by telephone in their six-room apartment on the twenty-eighth floor of the Waldorf Towers in New York. On the evening of the following day, the Windsors held a press conference in the Verandah Grill on the sun deck of the Cunard liner, *Queen Mary*, surrounded by gum-chewing reporters, photographers and cameramen. Around them were impressionistic decorations of acrobats, ballet dancers, a witch and her cauldron, and a cat. It was, as one observer commented, 'the most macabre setting in which British royalty can ever have appeared.' The Duke journeyed back to London alone— neither the widowed Queen nor David and Bertie's mother, Queen Mary, were prepared to tolerate the presence of Wallis. Weeks after the funeral, the Queen Mother was to refer to her as, 'the woman who killed my husband.'

The late King, described in the *Daily Mirror* as 'by any standards, anywhere, a good man', lay in State in Westminster Hall. His mother, sister and older brother went to pay their respects. The Duke of Windsor dropped on one knee as he entered and left the Hall, but otherwise showed no emotion. Bertie was buried in St George's Chapel, Windsor, awash with flowers from the famous to the unknown, Fulham street traders sent their tokens of respect as did Churchill—in his case a wreath in the shape of the George Cross which bore the words at its centre, 'For Gallantry'. The Queen Mother's tribute of white orchids, lilies and carnations, said simply, 'For my darling Bertie, from his always loving Elizabeth.'

While many had perceived the Queen Mother as being stronger than her husband, it now became evident that this was far from the truth. Lady Cynthia Colville, long-time friend and Woman of the Bedchamber to Queen Mary wrote, 'Few people realized how much she had relied on *him*—on his capacity for wise and detached judgement, for sound advice, and how lost she now felt without him.' As the Queen Mother was to say, when praised by admirers for her accomplishments. 'It was not me, it was us together.'

There were now fears that the Queen Mother would retreat from public life to the northernmost tip of Scotland where, in the first weeks of her widowhood, she had bought the derelict Castle of Mey. However, Sir Winston Churchill persuaded her that her duty remained with her family and the nation. While many years earlier, she would have distrusted his judgement, the Second World War had bonded a close friendship and she now felt inspired by his words. Her daughter, the new Queen sent her a red leather dispatch box embossed in gold with 'HM Queen Elizabeth, the Queen Mother', and ensured that she was eligible to serve as a Counsellor of State during the Sovereign's absence. The message was clear.

Only three months after the King's death, the Queen Mother fulfilled her first public engagement, saying farewell to her own regiment and that of her brothers, the Black Watch, as they left to fight in Korea. A few weeks later she surprised the territorials of the regiment when they came across her, at five o'clock in the morning, during a route march. Backs were suddenly straightened and shoulders squared as they spotted through the mist above Balmoral Castle their Colonel-in-Chief, complete with corgi, wrapped in a thick woolly overcoat and old felt hat. She was back on duty and in character. As Bertie would have wished, she was soldiering on.

Her father's death also left a terrible gap for Princess Margaret. 'Life seemed to stand still when Papa died. I cannot believe that I will grow old without seeing him again.' Now sleep was difficult and her appetite, always slight, was next to nothing. This had been her first real encounter with death and in her lonely suite at the opposite end of the Palace to that of her mother, who was also totally isolated in her grief, Margaret felt the full pain of the parting. Her calm and supportive older sister was absent, preoccupied with taking on the affairs of State and her own young family. So she turned increasingly for comfort and friendship to the Queen Mother's new

Comptroller, Peter Townsend. Newly divorced, he found in the young Princess a sympathetic ear for his troubles and within a year, had confessed that he was in love with her. 'That is exactly how I feel, too,' she admitted.

The couple were discreet, talking while walking on the hill or riding together in Windsor Great Park, but the tiniest of gestures after the new Queen's Coronation was to make their romance public. As they waited in Westminster Great Hall, a radiant Princess cut through the throng and, like a wife, brushed a small speck of fluff from his uniform. The body language was obvious—they were in love, and the world now knew it.

Princess Elizabeth, now the new Queen, had known for some considerable time how her sister felt about Group Captain Townsend. While she bottled up the terrible premature loss of her father, she had to confront the first crisis of her reign. For once her mother, who was grieving the loss of her husband, was of no help. She had her own problems and the decision was up to others. As one courtier recalled, 'Queen Elizabeth did not see what she did not want to see. She left it to others to deal with the situation. Matters were now out of her hands.'

As Defender of the Faith and temporal Governor of the Church of England, the Queen, according to a close courtier, 'Hid her head in the red boxes.' She did not want to hurt her sister. But, weighed against this were the duties and responsibilities that she had learnt from her grandmother, Queen Mary, and from her father. She was determined, she said, 'that she would *never* let him down.' Meanwhile her sister was saying bitterly. 'You look after the Empire and I will look after my life.' In her distress and perhaps out of spite, Margaret suggested to her sister that she might care to take a closer look at Prince Philip's 'private' social engagements. The thought was to lurk in the Queen's mind for some time.

As a senior courtier later said, 'The Queen simply could not bear it. She buried herself in her work and hoped the situation would go away. She loved her sister but everyone was telling her that any marriage was impossible.' Shrewd as ever, the Queen Mother eventually came up with a solution—a 1,500-mile tour to Rhodesia. Meanwhile, Townsend was dispatched to Brussels. For two years the Princess and Group Captain Townsend were kept apart and did not meet.

In August 1955, Princess Margaret turned twenty-five and was free to marry without royal consent. However, the terms of such a union were onerous. Not only would she lose her rank and her £6,000 a year allowance but she would probably have to live abroad for a while. It was generally considered that marriage to Townsend would weaken the link with Commonwealth countries and that, at home, it would create a difficult position between the Crown, the Church and the Government. The Queen Mother was definitely against the match and she was more rigid in her attitude than the Queen. She had been trained by Queen Mary, and just as her mother-in-law had put duty before love at the time of the Abdication, so did the Queen Mother now. 'Would her father King George VI have approved of such a marriage?' she asked Princess Margaret. The answer was clearly not. The Queen Mother had seen her husband die because of the value he placed on duty, now she could point out to her youngest daughter where her duty lay.

'She was immensely understanding during the Townsend affair,' says a former aide. 'She has always had sympathy. She is not one to go rushing into angry speeches. She will listen and sympathize and not dictate at all. She will just try to quietly lead whoever is in trouble on to the right path. It is significant that when Princess Margaret announced that she would not marry

Peter Townsend, she did so from under Clarence House's roof.' As Princess Margaret was ruefully to remark. 'When you're royal, not even your love is your own.' This comment from the young Princess was to prove particularly poignant in her own life.

CHAPTER FOUR
SPECIAL RELATIONSHIPS

The shocking death of Diana, Princess of Wales, on the last day of August 1977, plunged the Royal Family into the greatest crisis it had experienced for over sixty years. Not since the abdication of King Edward VIII in 1936 had the throne rocked more precariously as the public turned its face against the monarchy in the days of hysterical grieving that followed the tragic Paris car crash. For the first time in her reign, the Queen felt a cold shiver of unpopularity as the entrenched traditions of the Palace proved too inflexible to respond to the mood of the nation. The Royal Family was perceived as uncaring as its members hid their personal feelings behind a well-worn mask of majesty while others, including Prime Minister Tony Blair, spoke in emotional terms about 'The People's

Princess'. This was a catch-phrase that would come to embody the Princess's life and a mantle that the monarch, albeit belatedly, would try to take on.

One of the most potent symbols of the gulf between the Queen and her subjects, and one that enraged even her most loyal supporters, was the absence of a flag flying at half-mast above Buckingham Palace. As official buildings throughout Britain demonstrated this mark of respect for Diana, courtiers explained in vain that protocol dictated that the royal standard could not follow suit. At a time of national mourning, when the public looked to her for leadership and mutual support, the Queen was absent, on holiday and out of sight behind the walls of her Scottish castle, Balmoral. To the tearful crowds surging up the Mall, clutching the flowers that they were to lay at the gates of her London residence, it was incomprehensible that the Queen they had so long respected appeared to care so little for the

Princess they loved.

The lessons of that time have been well learnt. Gone are the days when One was surrounded by One's pals and a discreet word in an editor's ear would still stop press attention. Increasingly, the royal 'firm' is becoming like any other Department of State, complete with spin doctors, special advisers and highly paid press officers. The modern ways and means of Government now prevail in the red plush corridors behind the Palace's formal Victorian façade.

How different might it have been if that other 'commoner', Queen Elizabeth, the Queen Mother, also an earl's daughter and not a princess of the blood royal, had stood in her eldest daughter's shoes during that troubled time. A forerunner of Diana, it was she who first brought a breath of fresh air into the stuffy formality of the court of King George V. It was she who pioneered the first walkabout and it was she who first spoke to people in language that they could understand.

Indeed, according to Dame Barbara Cartland, she once addressed a man earnestly about his bicycle—to his utter astonishment. Such a down-to-earth attitude allied to her charismatic charm, might have meant that she sidestepped the pitfalls into which the unfortunate Queen so innocently and unknowingly fell.

However, the Queen, despite her many gifts and undoubted qualities, cannot be like her mother. While the Queen Mother is a natural extrovert, who announced as a very young child that her hobby was 'liking people', the Queen finds it difficult to show her feelings and retreats behind a distant formality, which makes her appear cold. Never was this better illustrated than when she and Prince Philip returned from a long foreign tour and were met at the station by five-year-old Prince Charles and three-year-old Princess Anne. Mother and son exchanged a handshake but from Grannie there was a huge hug. As a former courtier explains. 'She [the Queen] had been trained like a trooper never to show her feelings and she is by nature a fairly undemonstrative person. She was a good parent in that she was absolutely fair and very consistent. The children always knew exactly where they stood with her and she was very firm. But she failed as a parent because she was unable to show emotion. She never found it easy to hug her children; in fact, she wasn't a woman for hugging at all. She never indulged them in any way and as for crying—that was definitely out.'

It was a very different story when Prince Charles and Princess Anne went to see their grandparents. In the words of a close friend, King George VI and Queen Elizabeth 'spoilt them to death. In their eyes they could do no wrong. Prince Charles was the apple of the King's eye—the longed-for son he had never had.' Godfrey Talbot, the BBC's Court Correspondent from 1948 to 1969, asserts that 'it was generally believed that Prince Charles was better for Grandpapa's health than any amount of medicine'.

When the Queen went to Malta for a holiday with her husband, then an officer in the Royal Navy, Charles and Anne were left behind with their grandparents. During their stay, their grandfather wrote to his daughter; 'Charles is too sweet, stumping about the room. We shall love having him at Sandringham. He is the fifth generation to live there and I hope he will get to love the place.' Christmas brought two white tricycles, presents from their parents, which despite the weather, the children could not wait to try out. 'They were riding through the large state rooms of Sandringham House, ringing their bells and shouting "Fire, fire" at the tops of their voices. Queen Elizabeth asked them to stop and come and meet the guests,' recalls a courtier. '"Oh no, we can't do that Grannie," said Prince Charles, "There's a fire you see and we have *got* to put it out." Far from being cross, Queen Elizabeth just laughed.'

On another occasion, Princess Anne begged to be allowed to go to church with the rest of the family. Her request was naturally indulged but she was warned that she must behave absolutely perfectly. 'All went well until the congregation was solemnly kneeling to say the prayer for the Royal Family,' remembers a fellow guest. 'As we were all calling on God to bless and protect Philip, Duke of Edinburgh, Charles, Prince of Wales, and other members of the Royal Family, Princess Anne, much to her brother's embarrassment, leapt to her feet and yelled at the top of her voice, "Duke of Cornflakes" before bursting out laughing. Naturally, she was hustled out of church but we were all quite surprised that she didn't really get into trouble.' Prince Philip, however, was not amused. 'He used to complain to his wife that her parents were much too soft with the children and they were getting out of hand.'

The King's death brought Prince Charles and the Queen Mother even closer together. 'From the moment the King died, the Queen didn't have a minute to spare. She was plunged straight in at the deep end and immediately had to take over all the responsibilities of state,' recalls Mr Talbot. 'She had been trained since the cradle by her father that duty came before everything, including family. She reluctantly had to abandon her children and they virtually didn't see their parents for months on end. It was very upsetting and bewildering for the little boy, and he turned to Grannie for a shoulder to cry on. During the first years of the Queen's reign, the Queen Mother was both mother and father to them. In the full family sense, she took over domestically.'

Although two years younger, Princess Anne's attitude to her grandmother was more robust and she seemed to take the changes in her stride. Always the tomboy, she seemed the older of the pair and was the first to climb trees, ride ponies and whizz round on scooters. As their nanny, Mabel Anderson, remembers, 'He was never as boisterous or noisy as Princess Anne. She had a much stronger, more extrovert personality. She didn't exactly push him aside, but she was certainly a more forceful child. She was better with her hands, while Charles was all fingers and thumbs. She was always the ringleader and up to every sort of prank you can think of. Charles just tagged along.' A family friend recalls that when they were each given a pair of boxing gloves Prince Philip had to confiscate them because Charles 'seemed to be getting the worst of it.'

The young Prince and Princess loved staying with the Queen Mother in the informal atmosphere of Clarence House or Birkhall in Scotland. 'Her door was always open. She loved them joining her in the drawing-room for tea round the fire and then playing games.' says Mr Talbot. 'She made everything very cosy and homely which was just what they needed.' It was the Queen Mother who first awakened in Charles a love of music. 'She used to take him to the odd concert as a treat and he would sit there mesmerized. It was the outing that he particularly looked forward to,' he adds. The pair would also spend long days on the River Dee where the Queen Mother introduced him to her favourite sport, fishing. Even today, her grandson will travel as far as Iceland in the hope of landing a large salmon.

Of Prince Charles the Queen Mother once said: 'He is a very gentle boy, with a very kind heart, which I think is the essence of everything.' And he has described Grannie; 'Ever since I can remember, my grandmother has been the most wonderful example of fun, laughter, warmth, infinite security and, above all else, exquisite taste in so many things.' But life at home was very different.

As a friend of the Royal Family noted, 'Like many other aristocratic families, the Queen and Prince Philip chose to bring up their children in the traditional way. Offspring were definitely to be seen and not heard and the youngsters were firmly in the charge of Nanny. The children might see their parents at breakfast time or perhaps be summoned to the drawing-room for tea but like many others their daily lives were behind the green baize door. It was in many ways a typical Victorian upbringing, Mummy was a remote and glamorous figure who came to kiss you goodnight, smelling of lavender and dressed for dinner. Prince Charles worshipped his mother, the Queen—but from afar.'

To make matters worse, while Princess Anne's high spirits endeared her to her father, Prince Philip's relationship with his son was never good. 'He was the antithesis of his thrusting, sure-of-himself father and sometimes a disappointment to him. While he respected him, he was also in awe of him. The Duke's near-Teutonic orders and demands frightened him and made him more reticent,' recalls a courtier. 'It was really a vicious circle. The more exasperated the Duke became, the more he [Charles] went back into his shell.' His governess, Catherine Peebles—nicknamed Mispy (for Miss P)—noticed the same tendency. 'He liked being amused rather than amusing himself. He was very responsive to kindness, but if you shouted at him, he would draw back into his shell for a time and you could do nothing with him.' The Queen tried to intervene in the friction between father and son but it was really no good. 'They were just incompatible,' says a courtier.

Prince Philip taught his eldest son to sail but it was not a success. As Prince Charles recalls. 'I remember one disastrous day when we were racing and my father was, as usual, shouting. We wound the winch harder and the sail split in half with a sickening crack. Father was not pleased. Not long after that, I was banned from the boat after an incident cruising in Scotland. There was no wind and I was amusing myself taking potshots at beer cans floating around the boat. The only gust of the day blew the jib in front of my rifle just as I fired. I wasn't invited back on board.'

'I wasn't made to follow in my father's footsteps in any sense or in any way', Prince Charles ruefully admits. So it was that he turned to the only other close male member of the family, his great-uncle Earl Mountbatten of Burma, Prince Charles christened him 'my honorary grandfather', a compliment indeed if one remembers how much he loved his real Grandpapa, and he became the son the Earl had always longed for but never had.

Dame Barbara Cartland, a lifelong friend of Lord Mountbatten, noticed that Prince Charles 'always seemed to be the odd man out' in the family. 'It was a terrible shame because he was such a nice, gentle boy but Princess

Anne's strength of personality eclipsed him. She was so outgoing that she almost demanded to be the favourite.' According to Dame Barbara, Lord Mountbatten was desperately worried that the Prince of Wales was so introverted and so unhappy at school. 'Prince Charles was always rather a loner and Dickie tried to bring him out of himself. They would talk about absolutely everything. The fact that Prince Charles didn't get on very well with his father made Dickie all the more important. There is no doubt that Dickie treated him like an adored son.'

Dame Barbara says that Lord Mountbatten tried to intercede with the Queen on Charles's behalf. 'No one ever found out that the Queen used to come down to Broadlands (in Hampshire) to ride with Dickie at weekends. He sometimes used the opportunity to talk to her about his anxieties over the Prince of Wales.' When Charles came to stay it was a morale-boosting exercise. 'Dickie used to tell him how wonderful he was, encourage him to see things from a different point of view and to treat life as a joke.' Another friend recalls Lord Mountbatten 'larking about' with the Heir to the Throne. 'They shared a common, almost Goonish, sense of humour. I will always remember Lord Mountbatten, his black labrador Kimberley at his heels, teasing Charles that he hadn't got his £1 entrance fee ready when the pair of them were at the opening of Broadlands to the public.'

However, the Queen Mother took a somewhat less rosy view of the Earl. As the Queen once told a friend, 'Mummy has never forgiven Dickie for introducing David [King Edward VIII] to Wallis Simpson. She has always felt that the burden of being King was responsible for my father's early death.' Lord Mountbatten's late private secretary, John Barratt, went further: 'On account of his association with David, I believe the Queen Mother was always wary of him. They greeted each other cordially, and before his death she even visited Broadlands, but they were never comfortable together, I believe that, even in her old age, Queen Elizabeth felt betrayed by the Duke of Windsor, who so summarily propelled her ill-prepared husband to the throne. She was also aware that she and Bertie, before he became King, were never part of the glamorous set in which David and the Mountbattens moved, and I think she always felt a resentment towards them.'

When Lord Mountbatten's wife, Edwina, died and, at her own wish, was buried at sea, the Queen Mother remarked acidly, 'Poor Edwina, she always did like to make a splash.' But there was more to it than this. A senior courtier explains that the Queen Mother 'was very suspicious of Lord Mountbatten's motives. He had successfully engineered the marriage between the Queen and his nephew, Prince Philip. Now he was turning his attentions to finding a suitable bride for

Prince Charles and was pushing the cause of his granddaughter, Amanda Knatchbull, very hard. He very much wanted her to be the next Princess of Wales.'

The Earl had laid his plans well. When Prince Charles brought his latest girlfriend Camilla, later Parker-Bowles, to stay at Broadlands, his 'honorary grandfather' was emphatic. 'Have fun with her by all means,' he counselled, 'but for God's sake don't get involved. She's far too common. You could never marry her. The country wouldn't have it.' The lovelorn Prince dithered and went off to Canada to consider these weighty words. By the time he came home, Camilla had got fed up with hanging around waiting for him to make up his mind and had married someone else. 'He was heartbroken but it was too late,' remembers a courtier.

The way was now clear for the Earl to pursue his dynastic ambitions. If he was to turn a childhood friendship into a romance, Lord Mountbatten was well aware that the inexperienced Amanda, with her ethnic off-the-peg clothes, would have to be transformed into the type of polished, sophisticated lady that the Prince found attractive. In great secrecy—for her parents, Lord and Lady Brabourne, would have been furious if they had known what he was scheming—he sent her off to Paris to buy designer outfits and get her hair done—and he then despatched the pair to the Bahamian island of Eleuthera. Prince Charles dutifully proposed but Amanda only laughed and said, 'What a funny idea'.

According to John Barratt, 'Lord Mountbatten began to get tough with the Prince'. He bombarded Charles with letters, pointing out 'that no girl, not just Amanda, would be thrilled at the prospect of becoming Princess of Wales. It was asking them to give up a lot, and the rewards would not necessarily compensate for the loss of privacy.' Charles was surprised at this and promised to try harder.

In 1979, three months before he was assassinated by the IRA, the Earl was picking out presents for Charles to give Amanda and was planning for them to meet during Prince Charles's tour of India. He would naturally be there to push things along. 'It was going to be Lord Mountbatten's ace hand; he thought that if he could get the two of them together, relaxed and away from pressures, for at least some of the time, they would be drawn even closer. He was quite confident that the magic of India would do the trick,' reports his private secretary.

None of these machinations was lost on the Queen Mother and her distrust and dislike for the Earl gradually increased. 'They met very rarely,' says a senior courtier 'but when they did, they were very cautious of each other. They circled each other like the opponents they were—there was no warmth, no love lost.' Unlike Lord Mountbatten, Queen Elizabeth certainly did not believe in arranged marriages and was somewhat relieved when the relationship, such as it was, fizzled out after the Earl's assassination.

By now, no one in the Royal Family could escape the fact that there was a problem with Charles. The girls he fell for had been out in the world too long and if any one of them had been chosen as a bride, the media would have had a field day. Contemporaries remember him at parties making a bee-line for the shapeliest girl in the room and if there was a lot of cleavage showing, so much the better. 'He was naturally drawn to the extrovert tart-with-a-heart type,' a friend recalls. 'He really appreciated girls who were warm-blooded, cosy and overtly sexy. But they had to be a good sort, a good sport and fun to be with but never in a Sloaney snobbish way.' His favourite party games were passing oranges under the chin and a naughty version of charades. 'The trouble was that Charles's lack of affection during childhood spilt over into adult life. He found it hard to overcome his natural reticence and form good relationships with the opposite sex. Although very close to his grandmother, the Queen Mother, he found younger women hard work. He would either jump on them or be too shy to go near them. That's why he preferred experienced, confident, often older, women, who would take the initiative', he adds.

Thus there was a sigh of relief at Clarence House when the Heir to the Throne, now over thirty, called round one day and confided to his grandmother that he wanted to marry Earl Spencer's youngest daughter, the nineteen-year-old Lady Diana. She seemed the answer to their prayers beautiful, virginal and the offspring of a trusted royal friend. And the press and the people loved her. However, as a former aide remembers, 'Diana's grandmother Ruth, Lady Fermoy, the Queen Mother's chief lady-in-waiting, was completely against the match. She told the Queen Mother that she thought the couple were totally unsuited and that the marriage would end in tears. She strongly advised Queen Elizabeth to try to change Prince Charles's mind and dissuade him from going ahead with the proposal.'

But the Queen Mother was typically resolute in her reply. She told Lady Fermoy that she never gave advice unless it was asked for and that she thought Prince Charles was old enough and wise enough to make his own decision. 'If he is in love, and I think he is, and he wants to marry this girl then I will do all I can to help him,' she said, The Queen Mother was as good as her word. She took Diana under her wing and installed her at Clarence House. A former member of the household remembers being told, 'Diana had terrible doubts on the eve of the marriage but the Queen Mother managed to reassure her. She was terribly sweet to Diana—very understanding and very sympathetic.' It was the same story when her younger grandson, Prince Andrew, came to marry. Then she looked after his fiancée, Sarah Ferguson, in the days before the marriage.

However the Queen Mother is not quite the cuddly Grannie she appears—there is an iron fist inside the velvet glove. 'She is a very strong and tough character,' says a member of her household. 'We love her because it's clear to see that she is absolutely firm in her views and not someone to cross.' The Queen Mother has not only had famous tussles with Lord Mountbatten over Prince Charles but also with his nephew, the Duke of Edinburgh, over the way the monarchy should go. 'When the Queen came to the throne, the Duke was determined to modernize the Court,' recalls a senior courtier. 'The Queen Mother set her face against any reform or any change. She was frightened of what the Duke wanted to do. She thought, quite rightly as it has turned out, that by making the Royal Family more accessible, the mystery and respect surrounding the throne would be eroded. The harder the Duke pushed for change, the harder she applied the brakes. And the Queen was stuck in the middle, I remember the Queen once saying as we saw the car drawing up from Clarence House, "Well, that's where all the trouble is going to lie".'

The Duke and the Queen Mother were also at loggerheads over where Prince Charles should be sent to school. Both she and the Queen favoured Eton College, where all Queen Elizabeth's brothers had been. The Duke was determined that his son should go to his old school, Gordonstoun, as he felt 'the boy needed toughening up'. The argument raged back and forth but in the end it was the question of security that won the day. 'Eton is in a town and it was felt that there was a greater threat of kidnap than in a remote part of Scotland. In short, his parents thought he would be easier to protect if he went to Gordonstoun,' recalls a courtier.

It was a disaster. 'Prince Charles was completely shunned by the other boys who were afraid of being accused by their fellows of sucking up to the Heir to the Throne', recalls royal biographer Godfrey Talbot. 'He had a simply ghastly school life. He was miserable. It rather crushed him.' Instead of saying 'I told you so', Grannie went to see Prince Charles as often as she could and took him out for special treats. Even the Duke has admitted he was wrong. 'It is now acknowledged that he would have made friends if he had been sent to Eton because he would have been amongst his peers,' says a family member.

The Queen Mother's other grandchildren were never as close as Prince Charles had always been to Grannie. Princess Anne was a strong, resilient character who got on very well with her parents and led an independent and happy existence. Even her divorce from Captain Mark Phillips and subsequent marriage to Commander Tim Lawrence were handled with discretion and dignity. While the Queen

Mother was quietly supportive, she was never called upon to play a major role in Anne's private life.

The Queen's younger children, Prince Andrew (born on 15 August 1960) and Prince Edward (born four years later on 10 March), were lucky enough to enjoy a very different relationship with their parents. Although Nanny was always there to supervise the daily routine, the Queen was now a mature parent and an established monarch. After missing so much of Charles and Anne's childhood, she was determined to play a bigger role in the upbringing of her younger offspring. Even the Duke had mellowed and, in any case, he found he had much more in common with his younger, more macho sons, Prince Andrew took liberties with his mother that would have made his elder brother's hair stand on end. Ever one for a practical joke, he put itching powder in the Queen's bed and tampered with the royal television aerial. 'As you know the Queen is very keen on racing and once, when I was at the Palace, she turned on the television to watch one of her horses run,' recalls a friend. 'To her dismay, all we could see was a snowstorm. She was not amused and immediately summoned the engineer. He fiddled around for ages as she grew increasingly irritated. Finally, enter Prince Andrew with a big grin on his face. He thought the whole episode a great laugh and the Queen, after some protest, laughed with him.' The younger Princes love seeing Grannie—whether in London, Balmoral or Sandringham—but for them it is a more distant relationship. The Queen Mother was in her eighties by the time Diana, Princess of Wales, came on the scene. During the early days with Prince Charles, Diana, like other members of the Royal Family, paid court to the old lady on high days and holidays but as the marriage hit trouble, she suspected that perhaps Queen Elizabeth was not quite the ally she had supposed.

As royal biographer, Andrew Morton observes, 'Diana saw her London home,

Clarence House, as the fount of all negative comment about herself and her mother. She kept a distrustful distance from this matriarchal figure, describing social occasions hosted by the Queen Mother as stiff and overly formal ... At the same time the Queen Mother ... exercised an enormous influence over the Prince of Wales. It was a mutual adoration society from which Diana was effectively excluded.' 'The Queen Mother drives a wedge between Diana and the others,' noted a friend. 'As a result she makes every excuse to avoid her.'

It may be, however, that in the dying days of her marriage, the beleaguered Princess was being a little oversensitive. In the famous 'Squidgygate' tape, when a private conversation between Diana and her admirer James Gilbey was illicitly recorded by a radio ham, she talks about a 'strange look' the Queen Mother turned on her during lunch. 'It's not hatred, it's sort of interest and pity,' she said. Perhaps the Princess should have realized that there was more sympathy in that quarter than she imagined.

Even when the Queen Mother strongly disapproves, as she did when Diana and Fergie were photographed pretending to poke men's bottoms with their umbrellas, she very rarely says anything. 'It's the long silences and what she *doesn't say*, that really hits home,' observes a member of the household.' That's when you know you are in deep trouble.'

Today, events seem to have come full circle. Now Prince Charles is a single parent trying to help his boys, Prince William and Prince Harry, come to terms with their mother's tragic and untimely death. Despite being in her ninety-ninth year, Grannie is still there to lend a hand. As a senior courtier notes, 'I think she is the one person that he can be with and not feel he is under scrutiny. He is totally relaxed in her company because he doesn't feel he is being constantly assessed and judged the whole time. And I am sure that he tells his grandmother things he would never dream of telling anyone else and consults her about the boys. In the Queen Mother, he has always found sympathy and understanding—someone prepared to listen and who is not constantly trying to give him advice. The way the Prince of Wales took his grandmother's arm during the VE Day celebrations says everything about their relationship. It's a very special closeness indeed.'

CHAPTER FIVE

ON TOUR

From a very early age, the Queen Mother's character was such that she always felt an affinity and closeness to both her family and the people. The very small child who announced that her favourite hobby was 'liking people', was put in charge of showing guests at Glamis to their rooms as a youngster. As she mounted the ancient stone spiral staircase, she would chatter away asking questions about their journey and pointing out items of interest. And when she was only four years old her mother, Lady Strathmore, once found her entertaining visitors to tea in the drawing-room, having rung for it herself, after they arrived early and she was elsewhere. One senior politician was startled when he was earnestly addressed by a pretty, little imp. Indicating an alcove off the drawing room, she said, 'Shall us go and talk?' Their conversation, as far as he can remember, lasted for a full forty-five minutes.

When Elizabeth was a teenager, she mixed effortlessly with ordinary soldiers, many of them from overseas, whom she helped to nurse during the First World War. Later she accompanied her mother on her visits to the sick and old on the family estate. She always had ready a friendly word for everyone. She gave her first speech at the age of fifteen, at a jumble sale, and confidently met the King's daughter, Princess Mary, at the head of her platoon of Girl Guides. She was overawed by no one and loved by all.

Therefore, it comes as no surprise that when she married and became King George V's only daughter-in-law, she slid happily into her role of royal representative and public person. 'It was as if she had been doing it all her life,' one courtier remarked. The truth was that, in a sense, she had. She loved people, whoever they were or wherever they were from and, indeed, wherever she might be.

Her first foreign adventure had been as a child when she visited her maternal grandmother, Mrs Scott, in a villa above Florence before the First World War. She and her younger brother David never forgot the excitement of travelling through Europe on the night train and she was thrilled by the bustle of a typical Italian station. In the care of their maiden aunt, Violet, the children were taken to see the Pitti Palace, the Boboli Gardens, the trecento frescos and the Medici tombs. It was a trip she never forgot and was frequently to return to Italy in both a public and private capacity. Her second trip abroad came in her early twenties when she went to visit her old friend Diamond Hardinge, the daughter of the British ambassador in Paris. The pair took in all the sights and went up the Eiffel Tower. There was also a good deal of shopping and giggling. Her second trip to Paris was a sadder one. Diamond was dying of tuberculosis and Elizabeth Bowes Lyon was one of her last visitors.

On her marriage into the Royal Family, Elizabeth's horizons broadened as she was called upon to travel widely throughout Britain and abroad. Everywhere she went, her charm and wit made her friends as she smoothed her shy husband's passage through public engagements.

Never was her tact more needed than during the tour of South Africa in 1947 when the royal couple and their daughters spent two months travelling—and indeed living—on the White Train as they journeyed through the country. At one stop a grizzled old Afrikaner who had fought in the Boer War pushed his way into the line of local officials to be presented. Equerries and ladies-in-waiting held their breath as he growled at the Queen, 'I can never forgive the English for what they did to my country.' After the briefest of pauses, the Bowes Lyon blue eyes flashed, as she sweetly replied, 'Oh I do understand. We in Scotland often feel very much the same.'

The reasons for the tour were threefold. The country's prime Minister, Field Marshal Jan Smuts, the former Boer commander who fought so tenaciously against Queen Victoria, had come round to the view that monarchy could favourably influence public opinion and there was a general election coming up. The British Government felt such a visit would strengthen bonds with the Empire and Queen Elizabeth felt it would benefit her husband after the strain of the Second World War. It would also be a valuable experience for sixteen-year-old Princess Margaret and her older sister—a foretaste of what would inevitably become a major feature of their official lives.

Although the King was to say that the trip had done him 'a great deal of good', he was often irritable in the heat and it was only his wife's enthusiasm that kept him going. The thirty-six nights on the train were indeed gruelling with a start at 6.30am when 'a black gentleman would come with a wet broom and start cleaning the windows,' and by the end of the journey he had lost a stone in weight.

In Oudtshoorn, 'the four of us' as the King called the Royal Firm, went to an ostrich farm. The King was expected to snip the tail feather off one of the unsuspecting birds but at the crucial moment there was a loud squawk and he accidentally took a quarter inch off its bottom. The ostrich, its head still in a canvas sack, began to quiver as did the King. Smiling serenely, Queen Elizabeth came forward and, taking the scissors, delicately snipped a piece of feather off its behind. 'We do a lot of gardening at home,' she explained to the assembled company. 'The King is good at digging and weeding but it is I who concentrate on the secateurs.'

Despite fears that the Royal Family might receive a cool reception, they were mobbed everywhere they went,

Princess Margaret, already with a schoolgirl crush on her father's equerry, Group Captain Peter Townsend, was in fine form—her vivacity and 'presence' was not lost on the local press. Her older sister was described as shy and even grave—no doubt pining for her sweetheart Prince Philip whom she rang as often as possible from the White Train. However, she did rally, on the homeward bound leg of the journey, when, on her twenty-first birthday, she pledged that she would dedicate her whole life to the peoples of the Commonwealth, 'whether it be long or short.'

It was not Queen Elizabeth's first trip to Africa. During the first year of her marriage, repeated chest infections plagued her and schemes were suggested so that she could escape the bleak British winter. A journey to the heart of Africa was suggested, part official, part holiday. It was a thrilling prospect for someone who had spent her childhood pouring over the world atlas, Elizabeth and Bertie were all for the trip.

As they boarded the train bound for Marseilles on I December 1924, little did they realize that it was perhaps to be the greatest adventure of their lives and one they would never forget. Before they even arrived in Mombasa, Bertie had to undergo the double indignities of crossing the Equator twice, being shaved with a wooden razor and chucked into a tank of cold water.

Life was no less exciting as soon as they landed when they attended a ngoma or as one observer recorded, 'five thousand uncouthly bedizened natives dancing wildly for their delectation. As the participants had been prancing for three days their movements were by now somewhat rhythmically drunk and unorthodox. Some had gilt crowns bedecked with candles on their heads. In many cases a grass skirt was the only addition to the form in which they had been made. Tom-toms beat and horns howled.' As a memento the royal couple were given a gold coin on a red ribbon and an address thrust into the hollowed-out trunk of an elephant. Later they witnessed a march past of 12,000 Nubian warriors dressed only in monkey skins and attended a native parliament where the King invested King Daudi, the Kabaka of Buganda, with the KCMG.

Their trip was to take them through Kenya, Uganda and the Sudan, travelling 300 miles by train watching the game from a carriage in front of the engine, before embarking on a five-week safari. They were caught in a tropical storm in the middle of nowhere and seven of them had to pile into a Buick after one of the cars broke down in a river. They slept in little mud huts or under canvas or on the deck of a shallow draught steamer, which broke down. It was shades of the famous movie, *The African Queen* that was to star Katharine Hepburn and Humphrey Bogart in 1951. Elizabeth became an experienced hunter, shooting the plentiful game with a .275 Rigby, and went fishing on the Nile.

As her biographer David Duff records, 'Everywhere she had travelled her courage and tenacity had been admired. She had trekked fifteen miles and more at a stretch. She had been up to her waist in mud and water. She had helped put up her tent when it blew down and dried out her sodden clothes. She had shot for her supper. The praise, and the smile, of her echoed back from Mombasa and Nairobi, Entebbe and Khartoum.' It was a sentiment that was often to be repeated during the next seventy-five years.

The Queen Mother's warmth and regal informality was to become the template for her family on official duties. It was in Canada, just before the Second World War, that she first invented the royal walkabout. To the amazement of American newspaper men and the horror of her security guards, she plunged into a sea of 10,000 tough First World War veterans when she was unveiling a war memorial in Ottawa. Her five-foot-two frame disappeared in the throng as she was swamped by soldiers who well remembered her kindness and compassion to the wounded at Glamis. Perspiration poured from the protection squad as they struggled to keep in contact with their charge whom they could not even see. However, the Queen Mother was delighted with the experience. As banner headlines proclaimed that she had taken a risk that no other President or monarch would contemplate, her observation was merely that, 'Canada is so . . . so uplifting.'

She also gave her detectives heart failure by breaking away from the official programme. While laying a foundation stone, she heard the nearby burr of the Highland tongue. Realizing that many of the masons working on the building were from her native Scotland, she broke away from the group of

Canadian dignitaries and marched purposefully towards them, Bertie following in her wake. As 70,000 astonished spectators looked on, she stood laughing and joking with the workmen as they swapped stories of home. Such behaviour broke all the rules of royal precedent but it was a style that succeeding generations would emulate, most notably Diana, Princess of Wales, more than forty years later. It was no coincidence that, half a century on, it was to Canada that the Queen Mother returned, in her eighty-ninth year, for her last major foreign tour.

It was June 1939, when she left the United States of America for the last time before the Second World War, that the Queen Mother was first dubbed 'The Queen of Hearts', a mantle that Diana was also to adopt. Her famous smile and tireless energy attracted crowds of three million or more as she took the country by storm. More unfamiliar compliments were paid to her. She was described as 'A Cute Trick' and President Franklin Roosevelt confided to her husband. 'My, you're a great Queen picker!' When she returned to the country as a widow, it was the same story. As the *World-Telegram* commented, 'The royal lady with the peaches-and-cream complexion and the twinkling orbs not only drew a record crowd of 2,800 smart-setters to the Waldorf-Astoria ballroom; she sent them away humming "God Save the Queen" like a first-night audience whistling the top tunes of the hit show.' Negro children, whom she visited in Harlem, said she was 'A Wow' and everyone agreed. However, her tremendous popularity could have its drawbacks. When she tried to go shopping at Saks, the department store in New York, she had to rocket up and down in the lift to evade a pack of puffing well-wishers. Despite the pursuit, she managed to buy presents for her grandchildren, a magnetic bottle-opener and a game of Scrabble, for herself.

It was not the first time that a royal tour had taken on a slightly ludicrous note. One of Princess Margaret's private secretaries recalls the Queen Mother telling a story about when she and the Princess were visiting an exhibition in South Africa. When it was over, their host duly bowed low as she thanked him for such an interesting tour. As the doors slammed shut, the car pulled slowly away and the Queen Mother started to wave to the crowds of well-wishers. The official was still walking alongside. 'What a nice man,' she commented, 'seeing us off so kindly.'

The next time she glanced out, the man was still there, now trotting, waving and looking a little flushed. As the Rolls picked up speed, the man continued to keep pace, waving wildly and starting to go purple in the face. 'If he's not careful,' said the Queen Mother, 'he'll give himself a heart attack.' Then the penny dropped. The cavalcade came to an abrupt halt and the tie of the half-throttled official was extricated from the door. With typical thoughtfulness, enquiries were later made to ensure that the man was none the worse for his experience.

There were other slightly silly moments when the Queen Mother visited Venice in her mid-eighties. Since childhood she had seen 'Serenissima' as a distant vision from the train carrying her south to Florence. Now, she determined that at last she would see the place for herself. Her devoted daughter, the Queen, lent the Royal Yacht *Britannia* and a jolly party set off. The most important and difficult function for the British Embassy officials was to ensure that the Queen Mother had the racing paper, *The Sporting Life*, on her breakfast table every morning. Her staff, it was explained, needed to know how their fancied horses were doing. There was clearly, too, a hot line to a friendly bookie. As the Queen Mother wondered at the glories of St Mark's Cathedral, one member of her household was sadly seen tearing up betting slips after the voice in his earpiece had informed him that they had lost.

An extraordinary incident was to take place during the trip. By popular request, the Queen Mother agreed to vary the official programme and take an unscheduled gondola ride on the canals. Surrounded by gondola 'gun ships', packed full of security officers armed with the latest and most powerful sub-machine-guns, she set sail. However, no one in the last minute arrangements had banked on the low bridges and the stature of the *Star* newspaper's royal correspondent, one Andrew Morton. Well over six feet in his stockinged feet and rightly named 'Superman' by his fellow journalists, he bent as low as he could as she passed under a bridge and passed her 'One Cornetto'. The Queen Mother looked at the ice-cream with surprise, before it was grabbed from her grasp by royal staff, passed like a bomb down the line of officials and thrown to the unsuspecting security men. Everyone had their headline.

Significantly, one of her visitors on board the Royal Yacht was Dame Freya Stark, a pioneering voyager who had journeyed alone through Arabia in the 1930s, The Queen Mother, too, loved to travel and became the first member of the Royal Family, although the oldest of the 'Royal Firm', to circumnavigate the world exclusively by air. While top executives complain of jet lag, her stamina is legendary. 'Her powers of recovery after even the toughest tour are remarkable,' says an aide. 'It takes her about six hours.' On one occasion she bettered this—arriving at the races only three hours after landing from a transatlantic flight.

Her great friend Lord St John of Fawsley well remembers her trip to Venice. 'We had had an incredibly tiring day visiting Torcello and in the evening there was to be a reception on the Royal Yacht. The rest of us were exhausted, but there she was greeting every single one of the three hundred guests. By the end of the party, I was slumped in a corner—but to my amazement, I saw Queen Elizabeth saying goodbye to all those same visitors.'

Another friend recalls a visit to her couturier. 'I remember when she came for a fitting after a long tiring afternoon visiting the Chelsea pensioners. She was asked if she would like to sit down and rest for a moment. 'Oh, no,' she replied. 'I am quite fresh, thank you, but I *did* feel sorry for those poor, dear, *old* gentlemen.' Their average age was a mere seventy-five and she was over ninety.

The Queen Mother's clothes have been admired and copied everywhere but it was on a visit to France that she became a fashion icon. The tour had been postponed due to her mother, Lady Strathmore's death, and the royal designer Sir Norman Hartnell, had just two weeks to change all her outfits to white, one of the colours of mourning.

According to George Mitchison,

former managing director of the House of Hartnell, it was her husband, King George VI, who was the inspiration behind the wonderful creations that were to evolve into her distinctive style of dress. 'The King took Sir Norman into the picture gallery at Buckingham Palace and, stopping under the famous Winterhalter portrait of Queen Victoria and her family, he pointed at the wonderful crinolines and said, "That is how I would like my wife to be dressed."'

The fashion-conscious French were bowled over and hundreds of column inches of newsprint were devoted to her dresses. And if they liked her clothes, the Parisians were no less rapturous about her person. 'Today France is a monarchy again,' screamed the headlines. 'We have taken Elizabeth to our hearts. She rules over two nations.' However, seeing how much she helped her shy husband, they could not resist a little joke at their expense. The Queen Mother was dubbed 'soutien-George', meaning George's support. ('*Soutien-gorge*' is a bra in French.)

'Her style has really evolved from there,' says Mr Mitchison. 'She has always favoured pastel colours, not only because pink and blue happen to be her favourites, but so she can easily be seen in the crowd. And she loved embroideries on the ball gowns we made for banquets and special State dinners. She used to explain that if she was sitting next to someone who was rather shy, she could use the embroidery as a talking point to get the conversation going. Her Majesty is a very discriminating customer. She has a firm idea of what she wants and we had to produce a lot of sketches. If she were going abroad, the outfits had to match the colour of the ribbon of whatever decoration she would be wearing and the dresses designed accordingly. I remember she used to point to a sketch and say, "Ah, I see there is room for a little tinkle there," meaning a brooch or a small piece of jewellery.'

In Britain, the Queen Mother still brings a touch of magic to whatever she does, although old age now prevents her from fulfilling the number of engagements she did in past years. The occasion, only a few years ago, will always be remembered when she turned the apparently dull task of viewing building developments in the regenerated Docklands area, into a triumph of public relations. Since the days of the Blitz, she has always loved the East-Enders and delighting in the atmosphere of a Cockney afternoon, she decided to join the locals in the pub. When her official duties were over, she instructed her chauffeur to stop outside a popular Stepney establishment and marched inside, surrounded by her entourage. The landlord and his customers did a double take as the familiar figure burst through the doors of the saloon bar. As soon as he had recovered his wits, the landlord offered her a glass of champagne. With the famous smile that has won her fans round the world, she declined his kind gesture. 'No, thank you,' she replied. 'Might I have a pint of bitter, please?'

For many years the Queen Mother was Chancellor of the University of London and one year it fell to the President of the Union to lead her onto the dance floor for the first waltz. The poor young man, who had two left feet, had taken a crash course in dancing lessons but the strain of the occasion took its toll. As he lumbered round the floor, sweating profusely, he found himself kicking his Chancellor all over the place. With a bright smile, and ignoring her crushed toes, the Queen Mother put him at ease and said, 'Don't worry, Mr President, you haven't knocked my tiara off yet.'

The Queen Mother is not one to stand on ceremony. On another occasion, she was invited for drinks at the university and to her host's horror, it was discovered there were no tongs for the ice bucket when she asked for a gin and tonic. With a smile and a twinkle in her eye, she said, 'Oh, Mr President, don't worry—we can manage like this' and putting her hand in the ice bucket, she extracted two cubes and dropped them into her glass.

None of her friends will ever forget the time when they were watching the racing in the royal box and the National Anthem struck up on the television. Her companions started rising to their feet but the Queen Mother waved them to stay put. 'Oh, do turn the set off,' she said. 'Unless one is actually there, it's rather out of place and embarrassing, don't you think? Rather like hearing the Lord's Prayer whilst one is playing canasta!'

The Queen Mother has been a public figure for over seventy-five years but she has never lost the knack of making people feel that she is just one of them. Not only is she adored by the public but has a lifelong love affair with the press. Unlike some other members of the family, she realizes that reporters and photographers have a job to do and she makes things as easy as possible for them. Many remember the old days when she would deliberately lead the King to a spot where there was the best possible backdrop and all recall her many kindnesses.

On one occasion a stray dog joined her on a platform and she bent down to stroke it. One photographer was reloading his camera and missed the shot. Seeing his distress, she called the dog back and did it all over again. Another time a petty official was pushing a photographer aside. 'Please don't do that,' she called. 'Mr So-and-So is an old friend of mine and we both have work to do.' However, perhaps one of the nicest stories is that told by royal photographer Ian Showell. 'I was the first man on duty outside Clarence House the day Lady Diana Spencer left the Queen Mother's home to marry Prince Charles. Shortly after I arrived at 4.30am, I noticed one of the curtains twitch at one of the windows inside the house. Soon afterwards, a uniformed footman came marching towards me bearing a silver salver laden with a teapot, a cup made of the finest royal china, plus milk and sugar, with the compliments of the Queen Mother. At that time in the morning, the tea tasted like nectar.'

CHAPTER SIX

A LIFE WELL-LIVED

The Queen Mother's legendary sense of fun frequently enabled her to use humour to dispel many an awkward situation. This was never truer than during a family holiday north of the border, as one of her great nieces remembers.

It was a cold, wet day in August. For what seemed like weeks the rain had been teeming down in Scotland and the grouse shooting season had been wiped out. With no guests at Balmoral because there were no birds to shoot, the family kicked its heels and waited for more clement times. An air of boredom and frustration hung over the castle. Then the Queen suggested that despite the weather, they might have a picnic in one of the royal lodges built by Queen Victoria and her Consort Prince Albert. The idea was enthusiastically embraced and instructions were given that hampers, dogs and children should be got ready.

The Land Rovers were packed, the family loaded and the convoy set off. Miles of muddy, potholed track separated them from their objective and the journey seemed to take hours. All became restive. Then, at last, the lodge was in sight. Everyone scrambled out of the cars and headed for the front door. But the front door was locked and who had the key? The family looked from one to another and recriminations began. 'I thought you told me . . .' and 'I never did' resounded through the air as the bedraggled, rain-sodden group squabbled about whose fault it was and who would take the long road back to fetch the key.

Suddenly, a large car drew alongside and the beaming face of the Queen Mother appeared at the window. An irritated Queen explained to her mother what had happened. 'Oh, my poor darling,' she responded. 'But I thought you were the Queen and all you had to say was "Open Sesame!"' Everyone laughed.

That impish humour, which she has been blessed with since childhood, is used not only to defuse tense situations, but also to tease. On one occasion the Queen Mother was entertaining her serious-minded, elder daughter to luncheon. The Queen very unusually asked if she might have a second glass of wine. 'Oh, my darling,' said her mother. 'Is that wise. After all you *are* the Queen and you have to reign all afternoon.'

Her younger daughter, Princess Margaret, has inherited her mother's wit. Major General Stuart Green, former Colonel of the Royal Highland Fusiliers, of which the Princess is Colonel-in-Chief, recalls a funny moment. 'I well remember the occasion of the Officers' Regimental dinner in Glasgow which marked the tenth anniversary of our merger with the Highland Light Infantry and the Royal Scots Fusiliers. Princess Margaret was naturally the guest of honour and we were sitting sedately at the high table. Suddenly a soldier, made bolder by a large quantity of whisky, came reeling out of the gloom towards us. It was quite plain that he was intent on addressing the Princess and was bound to say something ghastly. I had to do something about it and on the spur of the moment, I bellowed: "Go away and sit down." Luckily that deterred him and he went swaying off in the opposite direction. Princess Margaret turned to me with the sweetest of smiles and said, "Goodness me—the Queen is always saying that to her corgis and they never take any notice!"'

The Princess is not above pulling the leg of her 'Jocks' as she calls her Scottish regiment. A favourite joke is to ask one of the men a question when she is inspecting a parade. The answer is invariably concluded with the words, 'Yes, Sir.' 'But I am not Sir,' she will tease. 'I am Ma'am.' 'Yes, Sir,' will respond the flummoxed soldier. She is always very amused by that.

The exchange is typical of the Princess and leads to her mother's 'slightly eyebrows raised' attitude to her gifted younger daughter. 'The Queen Mother is only too aware that if they are, say, taking the salute at a military parade, Margaret will be standing very regally at her side but her sparkling eyes will be flirting with the chaps,' explains a former courtier. 'This leads to a very affectionate but rather distant relationship.' Her mother is also adept at handling the Princess's moods. Once, during a fire practice at Royal Lodge in Windsor Great Park, the Princess refused to get out of bed for a mock drill. The staff were dithering about what to do when they spotted the Queen Mother drifting down the stairs in swirls of chiffon. When told of the dilemma, she replied with a laugh, 'Oh well, she'll just have to burn then, won't she.'

Both the Queen Mother and the Queen share the same conservative standards and, despite a heavy load of public duties, centre their lives round the family. The Queen's face in repose can look rather severe but, as any of her courtiers will tell you, she is full of fun and an excellent mimic of the pretentious or pompous. She and her mother speak on the telephone every day and see each other as often as their diaries allow. 'The Queen loves her mother very much and she is frightfully important to her,' explains a former courtier. 'They have the same slightly mischievous sense of humour and laugh at the same things. They always have fun together and share the same interests, like racing. They both love the outdoor, country sort of life and prefer a long walk with the dogs to the social whirl. Because they had such a happy, secure childhood, the Queen Mother is very close to both her daughters and they are very fond of and loyal to each other,' he adds. 'And as some people have found to their cost, cross one and you cross them all.'

It was once suggested that the Queen Mother might be a very suitable candidate for Governor-General. The Queen was adamant in her reply, 'Oh no, I'm afraid not,' she said. 'We could not possibly spare Mummy.'

Never was this truer than when scandal touched the Queen for the only time in her reign. According to the famous correspondent Alistair Cooke, reporting from New York in February 1957, 'Not since the first rumours of a romance between the former King Edward VIII and the then Mrs Simpson have Americans gobbled up the London dispatches quite so avidly as they have been doing since Friday afternoon. For two days and nights the tabloid press and the evening papers from coast to coast have waved banner headlines over a story from London, first cabled to this country by the *Baltimore Sun's* London bureau, reporting a "rift" in the marriage of the Queen and the Duke of Edinburgh.' Unidentified members of café society were said to be 'talking openly' of an estrangement between the couple as Prince Philip made his way home following a four-month tour. 'Within twenty-four hours the Palace brushed off the rumour as "totally untrue",' continues Mr Cooke in his report. 'This prompt disclaimer was a disappointment to the scandal sniffers. But since the press here is united in the practising belief that where there's smoke, there's fire, no foreign news editor—from the most scurrilous to the most responsible—could ignore the story. Consequently the cables went out asking for "follow-up" stories. The only new surprise is the fact, which is the burden of today's dispatches, that the British press has by instinct or command submitted itself to a general gag.'

As a former member of the household recalls, 'The Americans thought they were on to a good thing. They had broken the news of Edward's love affair with Wallis, while the British kept mum, and they thought the same thing was happening again.

Unfortunately on this occasion, they could not have been more wrong. I was with the Queen at the time and she seemed not unduly fussed. In fact we made a few jokes about it. She realized, like the rest of us, that while the Duke, like every man in the world, loves a pretty face, things would never go beyond a gentle flirtation. As ever the Queen Mother was a tower of strength and advised the Queen to ignore the "silly rumours". She said it was very sad that some people had nothing better to do than indulge in idle gossip and hurt others. She was very protective and anxious that her daughter should not be hurt.'

Instead, with a supportive Princess Margaret at her side, the Queen Mother took the Queen off to enjoy a day's racing. 'She was determined that the family would present a united front and demonstrate how ludicrous the rumours were. Her judgement as ever was impeccable,' he adds.

Five days later the Duke was

bounding up the steps of an airliner, two at a time, to welcome his wife to Portugal. In the words of the *Sunday Express*, 'For two and a half minutes they greeted each other alone in a special compartment with the blinds drawn. Then they came out into the afternoon sunshine. The Queen was radiant. The Duke was smiling broadly. And on his tanned face was a tiny smear of lipstick.' Others noted that he was wearing a tie covered with hearts. All was well.

When Princess Margaret broke up with Lord Snowdon, she turned to her mother for help but found Queen Elizabeth even more distressed than she was. The terrible rows that went on into the early hours of the morning followed by days of silent sulks had taken their toll. The Queen Mother was very fond of Lord Snowdon and was upset when the couple finally parted. Also she worried at the depressed state of her daughter and was therefore pleased, although slightly surprised, when the

Princess found solace in the company of Roddy Llewellyn, fifteen years her junior.

Roddy was fond of entertaining the Princess at his commune in Wiltshire where upper class hippies emulated the 'good life'. The old Etonian, as the Princess's pet, was in turn invited to her mother's country home, Royal Lodge. One day the Queen Mother came face to face with the young man, wearing nothing but a pair of underpants, in a corridor. 'Oh, frightfully sorry, Ma'am' he apologized. 'I was just looking for nanny to see if she would be very kind and sew a button on this shirt.' The Queen Mother sailed majestically on.

The Queen Mother has always been a marvellous and generous hostess. The food she serves is always of the best and the wines, the finest. Friends look forward to an invitation to any of her homes because it is always tremendous fun, if at times a trifle exhausting. One guest remembers a dinner party at Royal Lodge. 'It was well past midnight and I had to get up at six the following morning to go to work. The party was still in full swing and Queen Elizabeth was on sparkling form. Toast after toast was being drunk, the raconteurs were in full flow and there were plenty of singsongs going on. I lent across the table and whispered to one of the ladies-in-waiting, "Do you think we might be going to bed soon?" "Have I got news for you," she replied. "This could go on until four in the morning." "Oh, my God," I gasped. "It'll kill me."'

According to one of her relations, the Queen Mother has an interesting attitude to drink. 'She does not consider champagne to be alcoholic and uses it as a pick-me-up. She normally has one or two stiff gin-and-its before she sets out on an engagement and wine with her meals. She is really incredible. Drink seems to have no effect on her at all.' Others too, she feels, should be fortified before official functions. One organizer was amazed when, shortly before they were due to take to the public stage, she proffered him her glass and said, 'Take a gulp.' While the Queen Mother seems to be always in the pink, some people occasionally feel a little bit the worse for wear the morning after. However help is at hand. A discreet little chemist's just up the road in St James's has a magic potion—commonly known as 'The Royal Hangover Cure'. The recipe is naturally secret.

At Royal Lodge there are lively musical soirées at which the Queen Mother herself has been known to perform. Accompanied by Lord Hailsham she would think nothing of singing popular songs like 'Sur le Pont d'Avignon' and 'My Old Man Said Follow the Van' as a duet with Noel Coward. She is fond of the theatrical world and she often entertains artists she admires at her London home, Clarence House. The opera superstar Luciano Pavarotti has dined with her. 'When I meet this lady, it is always such a great pleasure. She is the greatest lady in the world and I adore her,' he says.

The artist Sir Hugh Casson has visited her Sandringham home. 'There was a picnic on the beach at Hockham. The footmen brought up all the hampers and she unpacked them herself and set out all the food. After lunch she took the dogs for a walk. Not everyone went with her—some found it a little too brisk but she never seems to notice the cold.' The Queen Mother has always loved her dogs and she is often seen with her corgis sitting in an orderly circle around her. She gives each dog in turn a Good Boy Choc-drop, saying, 'One for you, and one for you, and one for you . . .' And when she has completed the circle, she pops one into her own mouth, with the words, 'And one for me.'

The Queen Mother likes anything that makes her laugh. One friend recalls an evening when the guests arrived terribly late. As they rushed in full of apologies, she replied, 'No, no, please don't be sorry. I was glad you were late because it gave me a chance to see *Dad's Army* again.'

The Queen Mother's stamina and tirelessness are legendary. According to Lord St John of Fawsley, nobody ever looks at their watch in her presence—to do so would be a mortal sin. 'If all is going well and everyone is enjoying themselves, time doesn't matter,' he explains. 'You never mention time in the Queen Mother's presence—because she is above time.'

Despite two hip operations, the Queen Mother's incredible energy is undiminished. On her ninety-eighth birthday she walked for fifty minutes greeting the crowds of well-wishers and accepting bouquets. As ever she had a kind word for everyone including one little six-year-old who blurted out, 'I have met your daughter and do you know, she is the *Queen!*' 'Yes, I know,' replied the Queen Mother. 'Isn't it exciting!'

Apart from her family, the Queen Mother has had two great passions in her life—fishing and racing. In both she has scored many triumphs landing prize fish from New Zealand to Scotland and winning many of the classics. About the only race to still elude her is the Grand National. Once she came very close, but her horse Devon Loch mysteriously collapsed with a clear lead only yards from the finish line. Although she reluctantly had to give up fishing in her eighties, she still loves nothing more than a day at the races surrounded by friends, many of them relying on her expert advice when chancing a flutter.

Every year she hosts racing weekends at Royal Lodge for one of her favourite events of the racing calendar, the King George VI and Queen Elizabeth Cup at Windsor. 'It's all very jolly,' says her cousin. 'We arrive on Friday evening in time for drinks and go racing all day Saturday. On Sunday we talk, or play bridge or racing demon. If the weather's fine, a game of croquet might be suggested.'

Although the Queen Mother has never bet on a horse, her long-time private secretary Sir Martin Gilliat used to love betting. It was an in-joke that whenever he backed a loser, he would turn to his employer and say, 'Well, there goes the car—we'll just have to go home by bus!'

The Queen Mother likes to keep up with weighing-room gossip and she is very loyal to her racing friends. One of her trainers, Nicky Henderson, recalls a dash to Clarence House so the Queen Mother would not miss a race. 'She was at luncheon at the Savoy where I had the honour of sitting next to her. I had a runner in the 3.10 at Fontwell Park and she quietly ventured, "Do you think we will be able to slip away in time to watch the horse? If you'd like to follow me . . ." I had visions of the royal party trooping into a betting shop, but no. I made my exit at 2.55 and jumped into a taxi I'd lined up earlier. When I told the cabbie, "Follow that Rolls", he thought he had landed a part in a film. We hurtled round Eros at eighty miles an hour and screeched through the gates at Clarence House. We rushed in, up the stairs, just in time to see the race on the satellite system. I only hope that I can move that smartly when I am ninety-four.'

Since childhood the Queen Mother has had a great love of thespians. According to a former actor she would ask if she might come down to the set while filming was going on. Therefore, she was on hand when *On Her Majesty's Secret Service* was being shot at Elstree. James Villiers, who was playing M to George Lazenby's Bond, was among the throng who showed the Queen Mother round the set. The actor is distantly related to the royal family and was on hand when he thought one of the cast was rude to her. With her usual aplomb, the Queen Mother shrugged off the incident, but he bellowed at the unfortunate individual, 'If twenty-four people die and I become King, I will have you beheaded.'

In the world of pictures, the Queen Mother, so carefully groomed by her artistic mother, is advanced by royal standards. She collects modern paintings. It was a great bond she shared with Sir Winston Churchill and she sent her friends copies of his book *Painting as a Pastime*. She began to collect paintings soon after she moved into Royal Lodge buying an Augustus John and examples of Wilson Steer and Walter Sickert. Later she added works by Monet, Matthew Smith and Paul Nash. During her husband's lifetime, she asked John Piper to make watercolours and drawings of Windsor Castle. King George VI was traditional in his taste. Noticing that the sky was stormy, he commented drily, 'What bad weather you must have had, Mr Piper.'

The Queen Mother's final public appearance will take place at Westminster Abbey where her royal life began on marriage in 1923. Although still in excellent health, with her usual common sense, she has planned her own funeral down to the last detail. She will occasionally pop into the Infirmary at the back of the Abbey to watch the ladies of St Faith, all voluntary and expert needlewomen, delicately repairing the Tudor roses on the royal funeral pall. And, with her exquisite good taste, she has made one final request. 'I am afraid that I don't awfully care for your candles,' she has told the Abbey's authorities. 'Do you mind if I bring my own?'

During her long and distinguished life the Queen Mother has witnessed as many changes as the century she has paralleled. When she was born, Queen Victoria was on the throne, people travelled by horse and carriage and the Boer War was still in full swing. Today Victoria's great-great granddaughter is Sovereign, advertisements predict that holidays will soon be taken in space and the major talking point in Britain is the Millennium Dome. She has come through two world wars and witnessed the rise and fall of Communism. She has seen the Court change beyond recognition and the world of her youth turned upside-down. Through all the trials and triumphs of her life she has been the bedrock on which monarchy and the nation has stood. She is the cornerstone of her family and the most adored grandmother in the land.

It is said that she once sent the beefeaters at the Tower of London into a spin when she asked to borrow the Koh-I-Noor diamond, the largest gemstone in the world. But the Queen Mother needs no such embellishment. She is the jewel in the Crown, her magic undiminished even in old age. The royal portrait painter Pietro Annigoni was asked why one of his best pictures was of her. 'It's because she has such inner beauty,' he replied. 'The Queen Mother is one of the loveliest people I have ever met. It is hard to imagine a kinder, warmer, more appealing human being . . . She is absolutely perfect.' Her family, the nation and the world would agree.

We hope you have enjoyed this Large Print book. Other Chivers Press or Thorndike Press Large Print books are available at your library or directly from the publishers.

For more information about current and forthcoming titles, please call or write, without obligation, to:

Chivers Press Limited
Windsor Bridge Road
Bath BA2 3AX
England
Tel. (01225) 335336

OR

Thorndike Press
P.O. Box 159
Thorndike, Maine 04986
USA
Tel. (800) 223-2336

All our Large Print titles are designed for easy reading, and all our books are made to last.